CONQUERING
ANXIETY

**Stop worrying, beat stress
and feel happy again**

THE Speakmans

CONQUERING
ANXIETY

**Stop worrying, beat stress
and feel happy again**

First published in Great Britain in 2019 by Orion Spring
an imprint of The Orion Publishing Group Ltd
Carmelite House, 50 Victoria Embankment
London EC4Y 0DZ

An Hachette UK Company

1 3 5 7 9 10 8 6 4 2

Every effort has been made to ensure that the information in the
book is accurate. The information in this book may not be applicable
in each individual case so it is advised that professional medical
advice is obtained for specific health matters and before changing
any medication or dosage. Neither the publisher nor authors accepts
any legal responsibility for any personal injury or other damage or
loss arising from the use of the information in this book. In addition,
if you are concerned about your diet or exercise regime and wish
to change them, you should consult a health practitioner first.

A CIP catalogue record for this book is available from the British Library.

ISBN (Trade paperback) 978 1 8418 8321 2
ISBN (eBook) 978 1 8418 8322 9

Printed and bound in Great Britain by Clays Ltd, Elcograf, S.p.A

www.orionbooks.co.uk

ORION
SPRING

Important Information before Reading this Book

This book is not a substitute for medical or psychological intervention, nor is the content intended to replace therapy, or medical help or advice.

While we are confident that this book will help to alleviate anxiety, and make a significant positive difference, there are no guarantees. We would therefore always strongly encourage you to speak with your doctor or a health professional about how you are feeling, and also to inquire about counselling or therapy.

Please do not be discouraged if you have already had therapy which to date has not been entirely successful for you. The success of therapy is very much based upon the skill set of the therapist who delivers it. It is often necessary, therefore, to speak to a number of therapists before meeting the one who fully understands your issue and is able to successfully help you.

Contents

Introduction

We are all masters of our own destiny and by picking up this book, you have made the first important step towards your recovery from anxiety.

By recognising and understanding that you are suffering from anxiety, you have moved closer towards the life you want and deserve – a life filled with inner peace and contentment.

We will guide you and be with you every step of the way, as you become emotionally stronger and return to having good mental health.

Together, we can address the causes of your anxiety and make sure you feel less anxious for the rest of your life.

Here's to an anxiety-free day!

Conquering Anxiety

In this book we will be sharing with you our approach to anxiety and anxiety-related disorders. We will also explain how anxiety starts, how to locate and challenge the cause of anxiety, and how this can help to manage or alleviate anxiety for good.

On a daily basis, we work with people who are suffering from anxiety, anxiety disorders and panic attacks. They are asking for our help, our advice, or just some guidance to help manage their feelings of anxiety. It truly saddens us that for many people, dealing with anxiety can be such a daily struggle – many people we see develop a fear of the fact they will have to wake up and live with anxiety every day.

Anxiety is a Symptom

Anxiety, and the feelings associated with anxiety, is not a cause but a symptom. From working closely with our clients and seeing anxiety manifest itself in every possible way, we have come to understand that there is always a trigger or several triggers that cause the negative symptoms associated with anxiety.

We believe that everyone is born free from anxiety and no one is destined to live a life consumed by anxiety. As a result, our life's work has been, and will continue to focus on, alleviating anxiety, negativity and sadness.

We hope that reading this book will help you to locate, challenge and address the thoughts and events that have created your negative behavioural references (known as 'schemas') and allow you to challenge and condition or change them, which will subsequently change your resulting behaviours.

But first we must understand where anxiety comes from.

What is a Schema?

The word 'schema' can sound rather academic, but it's simply a term used in psychology.

A schema is a cognitive framework or concept that helps organise and interpret information. Schemas allow us to take shortcuts in interpreting the vast amount of information that is available in our environment.

In simple terms, schemas are learnings that we acquire in our life. They can be both good and bad. If we have had a positive life, we will have an abundance of positive schemas, but if we have endured negative life events, then invariably we will have a plentiful supply of negative behavioural schemas.

Negative schemas are the culprits that cause feelings of low confidence, low self-esteem, anxiety and anxiety disorders such as phobias, obsessive compulsive disorder, panic attacks and post-traumatic stress disorder.

Schemas are the basis of all opinions, thoughts and beliefs, and depending on the age at which they were created, they can often be inaccurate and nonsensical.

We will continue to believe everything we don't challenge.

From a child's perspective

Most childhood schemas are naturally conditioned, or corrected, as we grow and mature. However, many remain unchallenged, particularly the schemas and associations created around an unpleasant or traumatic event.

We therefore continue to use an immature behavioural reference or schema that's stuck with a child's viewpoint.

This is often the case with phobias, or people with low self-esteem due to bullying during their school years.

As an adult, you may feel frustrated at the feelings you are experiencing that are due to a childhood schema which does not serve you, and this causes an internal conflict between the schema and your current thoughts and feelings. You know now that the schema is wrong or even ridiculous, but you just cannot override it and this makes you feel helpless. For example, if you have a phobia of mice, as an adult you know that the mouse cannot kill or hurt you, yet the moment you see a mouse you become hysterical, irrational or terrified: you become an adult acting like a child.

These childhood schemas often inhibit elements of your life, which can then lead to feelings of frustration and confusion. How you want to think, feel and behave is overtaken by how you actually think, feel and behave – behaviours that are based upon a thought process or set of circumstances from the past.

Challenging the Past

The good news is that negative schemas can be changed. We change them by conditioning them – essentially, challenging them with new and overwhelming evidence to the contrary. This process is the basis of our schema conditioning therapy.

As you read through the information we share with you and the case studies we have included for you to consider in this book, we hope we will help you to see your past negative schemas from a different, more positive perspective, and thereby alleviate the subsequent associated negative symptoms of anxiety.

By always seeing things in the same way, you will always feel the same way. Changing and upgrading your thoughts and perspective will change and upgrade your feelings.

> *Once you change the way you look at the world, the world you look at begins to change.*

The Path of Emotions

The two primal instincts are to survive and to procreate. These instincts keep the human race going. Sadly, there is no primal drive to make us blissfully happy, and herein lies the biggest problem we face as human beings.

> 'The most important decision we will ever have to make is whether we live in a friendly or hostile universe.'
>
> **Anon.**

We all have to accept that if we want to live a life of happiness, we have to create feelings of happiness from within. We then need to couple these internal emotions with external experiences and actions. We must practise continually – we have to work at being happy! But it's worth it.

Think of happiness like being physically fit. It is impossible to go to the gym once and then suddenly attain a toned and healthy body. Fitness is a process that has to become a lifestyle. Being happy and creating happiness is no different.

The Key to Upgrading Your Life ...
is Practice!

We are not born predisposed to be happy – positive emotions have to be cultivated and practised on a daily basis. Make no mistake: this takes effort. Social conditioning (how our society and environment train us to behave and what is considered to be acceptable among our peers) is slanted towards the negative. In essence, practising being happy is going against our nature, because really we're here just to survive. The good news is that happiness is attainable, and by practising daily techniques you can create a self-fulfilling happiness prophecy.

In our book, *The Key to Upgrading Your Life*, we created a comprehensive guide for how to think and feel happier. In that book we shared techniques on how to create new positive core schemas, as well as many tips and exercises to create happiness, and we explained the necessary components required, including our environment and our friends, and also challenging negative learned beliefs and behavioural references (schemas).

Our aforementioned book provides a good foundation to help counteract the daily challenges we all face, and it can help change your perspective in support of a friendly universe.

If we imagine our life measured on a 'scale of happiness', with positivity on one side and negativity on the other, we know that it is natural for us to move up and down the scale as we go through life. Irrespective of the negative challenges you may face in your day, our schema conditioning psychotherapy helps to add weight to the positive side of your scale, and also helps to lighten your perspective and approach towards negative events. With a more positive outlook, your levels of anxiety will decrease and refocus your mind on the present.

The Scale of Happiness

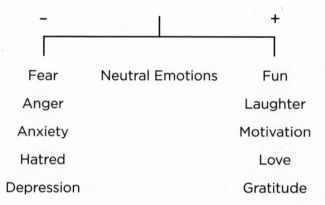

Fear	Neutral Emotions	Fun
Anger		Laughter
Anxiety		Motivation
Hatred		Love
Depression		Gratitude

If you consider the scale of happiness, the good news is that you cannot be at both ends at the same time. For example, you cannot feel afraid or angry if you are having fun and are laughing. Therefore, it is vital to direct ourselves to the positive side of the scale.

I have no idea what words to use to even start explaining how much you have helped me. Thank you so much for not only helping me conquer my fears, but for giving me back my smile. You have both absolutely changed my life. I will always be thankful to you both for how much you have helped me. Keep doing what you are doing. You are amazing.

Sarah

Again, happiness is not a birthright, genetic predisposition or created by luck. As well as challenging negative anxiety-causing schemas, which this book will help you to do, you also have to take positive steps to create positive emotions, such as spending time with friends who make you feel good about yourself, watching TV programmes or films that will make you laugh, practising gratitude every day and learning to love yourself.

A Fresh Perspective

As you read through this book, we will share with you our advice on how to alleviate and work through anxiety disorders. We've worked with thousands of clients and have seen every manifestation of anxiety – from quietly destructive to dramatically debilitating. And that's why we're in the best position to share our knowledge of what's worked for every kind of person.

When we have a fear, phobia, problem, negative schema, bad memory or traumatic event, we are immersed in it, and as a result it is difficult to see it from a different perspective. It's like drowning in negativity. You're blinded and paralysed by it.

We're sure that many times in your life, a friend has told you that their world is falling apart because of a huge problem, a problem they just can't get around. They tell you the full story and it's almost as if you are still waiting to hear the problem. Then, when they ask you what you think, you answer, 'That's not a big problem.' You can see a route out or a plan that will ease the pain of your friend, a plan they just couldn't see. And that's because when you are not emotionally involved in a problem, it is a lot easier to find a solution.

For this reason, not only will we share our approach to anxiety in the hope you can use it to help yourself, but we will also be sharing numerous case studies that will give you the opportunity to see someone else's issues from a non-emotional third-party perspective, thereby giving you an alternative point of view, and the formula we used to help that individual. We hope that you can then apply a personalised version of the same formula to work through your own problem and become less anxious.

Hope Can Shine through Anxiety

We very much hope you enjoy reading our book and find it helpful and informative, and the real-life stories and case studies inspirational.

You are not alone in your feelings right now, however deep your levels of anxiety are, and that's one of our most important messages.

So many people we meet in person, speak to or interact with on social media, have told us that seeing our work on television has given them hope and a reason to wake up each day. This is the greatest compliment we could ever receive, knowing that we have changed their lives for the better.

As you read our own personal stories of life challenges and anxiety, and the many people who believed they could never overcome their issue who we then subsequently helped, you will realise that there is always hope and always a reason to continue to search for or ask for help, until you have your answer that will release you from your anxieties.

1

Our Therapy

Since my therapy with you a year ago, I have experienced the greatest changes. It has been a fabulous year, and I have allowed myself to enjoy it. It is how I have been feeling inside where the greatest change is. I now feel I am truly worthy and deserving of love and happiness. I recently visited my brother. He and his wife were stunned by my transformation. They described me as having 'a shining aura'. You saved and transformed my life and are the most amazingly incredible people and therapists in existence. I had multiple and complex issues, but you healed me.

Liz

Our Conditioning Therapy for Anxiety

This book is about helping you. We really want you to have the closest experience possible to being in a session with us in person, and therefore we would like to start our journey together by explaining the basis of our therapy in a way that is personal to you, which you can identify with. Once you understand this, you can relax and know that we will share information and suggestions with you, to help you see things from a different perspective. Once you accept this new perspective, the way you look at the world will change, and in turn, the world you look at will change.

With that in mind, we would like you to imagine how you would feel if we told you we were going on holiday, and we would like to offer you a job looking after our pets while we were away (on the assumption that you, like us, are an animal lover!). We would pay you handsomely for the job, as we want nothing but the best for our animals. We introduce you to our six cats, showing you where and how they like to be fed, explaining that you need only call in twice a day to feed them. This all sounds straightforward.

We then escort you to a large enclosure in our back garden, and show you our gorilla, which also needs to be fed twice a day. We explain the enclosure's two-door safety policy, explaining that you have to go through the first door into a holding area, then close it before opening the second door into the gorilla's habitat. Bemused and a little nervous, you figure you can manage this task for the next seven days, and off we go on holiday, leaving you in charge of our beloved pets.

Although perfectly happy with our cats, you decide to google silverback gorillas and find that you may have made a hasty and rather dangerous decision. You start to regret agreeing to feed our gorilla when you discover that male silverback gorillas weigh 300–400 lb on average, and can reach speeds of up to 25 mph. They are also reported to be six times stronger than a human, with a bite force of 1300 lb/in^2: twice as strong as a lion! Nevertheless, having made your commitment to us, despite your discomfort and uncertainty you continue to feed our gorilla, but every feed makes you more and more anxious and fearful. Sometimes you have to wait hours for the gorilla to be at the other end of the enclosure before you can enter, giving you the best chance of getting out if it ran at you. Your sleep becomes affected as you worry about the fact you will have to go and feed the gorilla the next day, and this affects your appetite and general mood. Your anxiety and fear begin to consume you, as you feel after each successful feed that you are pushing your luck. You visit your doctor, explaining you feel anxious day and night. Because you have not mentioned the gorilla, the doctor assumes you have anxiety or generalised anxiety disorder.

Seven days later, much to your relief we return home from holiday, asking you how the week has been. You tell us, 'It's been horrendous. In fact, it has been without doubt the worst week of my life. I've been filled with anxiety, fear and dread every day at the prospect of feeding your gorilla, as it is a really dangerous animal that could easily have killed me.'

A little surprised by your comment, we gently ask you to follow us to the cage, and when we get there we ask you, 'Did you not speak to Pete?'

You look at us entirely confused as we call Pete to come over. As the gorilla approaches, we ask him to take off his mask, and you see for the first time that the gorilla is actually a man in a gorilla suit. We then explain that we have been conducting a social experiment with Pete living as a gorilla for a month. In that moment, your anxiety immediately disappears as you realise that you totally misunderstood the situation. With this new contrary evidence that we have supplied, your schema about the gorilla changes instantly and indefinitely. We don't ever have to remind you he's a man in a gorilla suit, and you don't have to go home and work on your anxiety, breathing through it or considering how to manage it. The link you had created between the gorilla and your fight-or-flight response has been severed entirely because of the new evidence you now have.

The inaccurate schema you had has been positively conditioned with the overwhelming positive evidence we provided. You never feel anxious being around Pete the gorilla again, and when we ask you to feed him in the future you do so with no anxiety whatsoever.

While this may sound like a silly metaphor, it is a great

example of how our therapy works and how you can change, without needing multiple meetings with us to keep asking Pete to take his mask off. Once your belief has changed, it alters how you feel. Every one of us has a number of our own anxiety-causing schemas, and we want to help you unmask your fear and anxiety-causing schemas, and positively condition your beliefs. Essentially, we want you to find and unmask your gorilla.

Our questionnaire

So, welcome to your first session with us. We all have 'gorillas' that cause anxiety and need to be unmasked. We may not even realise what exactly they are, so let us find out more about you. We would like to help you discover what life events may have created negative schemas that today contribute to your anxiety. Let us help you look for clues. We will also be asking you to consider the positive elements of your life, which we will ask you to consider once more when you have finished the book. You should see that more positive and happy memories begin to surface once they are released from the weight of negative past events.

Take a pen and paper, and write down your answers to the following questions:

* **Briefly describe your typical day. What you do and the people you surround yourself with will impact how you feel, so it is very important to consider this.**

* **What events, people or experiences have contributed to making you the way you are? Please be specific.**
   1. **Positive.**
   2. **Negative. As you read through the book, these are potentially the schemas you will need to address and challenge with contrary evidence. When you think of**

each negative experience, score your negative feeling out of ten. When you have finished the book, score each one again to highlight what has changed and what still needs to be worked on.

* What would you say are your biggest personal:

  1. Successes?
  2. Failures? When you have finished the book, note how each failure resulted in a positive learning.

* What is your specific reason for reading this book? Noting and rereading this every time you pick up the book will help you to look for a solution to this specific problem.

* When did this issue start? Knowing this will give you clues as to the time in your life when something may have occurred to create your anxiety-causing schema.

* What dreams and ambitions did you have when you were younger?

* What dreams and ambitions do you have now? This will help you to reflect on the things from childhood you may still like to work towards as an adult.

* List everything in your life that you appreciate.

* List the values and qualities you appreciate about yourself.

* Score your life out of ten. Please reflect on this again when you have read the book, and consider what else must happen and what actions you can take to make this score a nine or ten.

* If you could attempt any one thing and you knew that you couldn't fail, what would it be?

* Finish the sentences below, writing the first thing that comes to mind:

  'Life is a .... '

  'People are ....'

  'I am ....'

  'I need ....'

  'I wish ....'

  'If only ....'

* What is your most frequent recurring thought? This will give you an idea of what occupies your mind – this may also be creating anxiety, and so needs to be challenged with contrary evidence.

* List your top ten personal successes (e.g. passing your driving test, earning a degree, getting married, getting a job, organising a party, making someone laugh, an act of kindness).

* What comedians/actors makes you laugh? You can't always control external events but you can make time for laughter, and watching clips of these people will help you feel happier.

Your timeline

To feel happier today and in the future, it is important to feel happy about your past as well.

A great way to do this is to write a timeline of your life, so that you can look at negative events and positively change your perspective on each one, slowly and systemically.

It is equally important to be aware of all the positive things that have happened in your life, which should include your achievements, times you have laughed uncontrollably, been somewhere exciting, fallen in love; an amazing date, a fantastic concert, or other memorable events. You should read your positive events on your timeline regularly to remind you of the great things you have done, seen and experienced.

With regard to the negative list, you can work on just one event at a time, ensuring that you read your positive list before and after. To try and reduce the negative effects of each memory, it is important to find something to help you feel better about it. This may be acknowledging that you have learned something new from it, or that it made you stronger, more empathetic, kinder, or able to help somebody as a result.

Also consider if it is something that has been and gone, and is now over. If so, you are no longer a victim of that event; you survived it and you became a victor. Alternatively, you can change your emotional attachment to a negative event by accepting that it was not personal to you. For example, if you have experienced an abusive relationship, this was not instigated by you, nor was it personal to you – the abusive partner will have been abusive in the past and will continue to be abusive in the future. The abuse was not personal to you and it was the abuser who had the issue.

If after reading this book and considering the suggestions you are struggling to change a negative event to a more positive perspective, try speaking to a therapist or a positive friend that you trust. Explain to them that a painful memory is affecting you today, and ask if they could offer you any suggestions to be able to see the event in a more positive light, so that you can sever that emotional tie and leave the event in the past.

When you are starting to feel better about the event, move on to the next, so that systematically you can work through painful memories to ensure they have no negative effect, or a lesser effect, on you today.

Carrying the past is an unnecessary weight on your shoulders that does not impact your life in a positive way. Therefore, even if you find it difficult to lessen the negative emotion, you can start by making a decision to remind yourself that what you endured should not have happened, that you didn't deserve it to happen, but that it is now over. In any event, a timeline like this is a great tool to take with you if you are having or seeking therapy, as you can direct your therapist to all the areas in your past that you would like to work on to improve.

Now, please complete a timeline of your life events, using the template opposite. We send timelines out along with our therapy questionnaires to all our clients, and often we receive more than one page back – in fact, one lady sent us seventeen timeline pages, as she had so many life events to deal with. Bearing that in mind, do not worry how many pages you fill, as long as it allows you to find the answers you need.

Consider each negative event, and whether it still affects you or causes you any discomfort or anxiety. Score the negative event out of ten (zero means it has no negative effect and ten means you feel an extreme negative reaction).

If you have scored anything in the negative life event column as a six or above, this could contribute to feelings of

BIRTH

POSITIVE | NEGATIVE

NOW

anxiety and may have created negative behavioural schemas that affect you today. These are all events that need to be challenged to positively alter your perception, so as to condition the schema created at that time.

If you can see an event for what it really was and not how it felt at the time, this will allow you to become emotionally distanced from it. You can then become a third-party observer of that past life event, as opposed to allowing the memory to play in your subconscious and affect your present. You will notice, for example, that when your friends have a problem, while you may be upset for them, not having a personal attachment to the issue allows you to have no emotionality around it. Therefore you are able to soothe them and forget what happened. This is where we want you to be when you think about the negative memories you have.

You will see many examples as you read on, but to start you off right now we would like you to go through each negative event in your timeline and ask yourself the following questions, to begin to positively condition and alter the negative schemas:

* **Was it personal? For example, was someone mean to you specifically, or were they a person who was unkind to everyone? If so, the event was not specifically about you. Perhaps the person who made you feel bad had low self-esteem, or had a difficult upbringing, so they knew no different.**

* **Was it just an unfortunate accident?**

* **What did you learn? Did the event make you stronger, wiser, more compassionate?**

* **What good came from that? Did the event make you more charitable, more understanding of others?**

* **What actually happened? Describe what happened – factually and without emotion.**

None of us are immune from bad things happening, and we often get trapped in a past event without realising we had no control over it, and forgetting that despite that, we survived it.

Traumatic life events can often feel so personal and make us feel lonely and weak, but please know that you are not alone. We have all had life challenges – some worse than others – but take solace in the fact that you got through all your issues. You survived your worst ever day, and therefore you can get over any other issue too.

You may not be able to forget the event, but you can certainly change your perception of it, cut the emotional ties and leave your anxieties in the past. You deserve to be happy, and free from the burdens of anxiety. So, a very well done for taking the action needed to start working on improving your thoughts and feelings.

2

What is Anxiety?

I can't express how much my life has changed since meeting Nik and Eva in May this year! I had a huge fear of flying for over eleven years, and a fear of heights. After speaking with Eva at the event for five minutes my whole mindset changed. I went home, wrote down all my goals, and I am totally smashing them. My first goal was [to ride] the London Eye, which I achieved in July, and I got back a few days ago from Amsterdam. I fly to New York in October, and finally I have booked to fly to Florida with my family next year, something I have promised my two boys for a long time! Nik and Eva are truly lovely people and have a passion to help as many people as they can. Like they say, no one should live with any form of anxiety or unwanted behaviour, and I can honestly say I don't anymore.

Lindsey

Anxiety Levels

It's very important to remember, as we work through this book and your anxiety, that you are not alone in feeling anxiety. According to the World Health Organization, anxiety is 'a major contributor to the overall global burden of disease'. At present, anxiety is the widest cause of depression worldwide, according to the World Health Organization. And the figures are rising.

It's crucial to understand why our bodies create the sensation of anxiety, because doing so can help to reduce the negative impact we feel.

Anxiety is a general term for several disorders that cause nervousness, fear, apprehension and worrying.

Anxiety is a normal part of life. No one is immune from anxiety, although it can affect us all in different ways. Everyone will feel anxious about something at some time in their life, but it is not something you have to live with indefinitely or for every moment of every day.

Anxiety can be something that occurs as a one-off episode; for example, having a health concern or having to do a presentation. While those two things can make you anxious, once they are over the anxiety should go. Anxiety can also be something that persists for a longer period, again due to a known cause – perhaps as a result of job worries that consume your daily thoughts. But in clinic, we are seeing a lot more sufferers who do not know the cause of their unsettled, anxious feelings.

Anxiety can be persistent, frequent or occasional, and for many it can be completely overwhelming, making it difficult to manage everyday life. Many sufferers can inflate and exaggerate situations which others consider normal events. For example, a person with claustrophobia may become anxious at the thought of leaving their home, as the idea of being in a car, a toilet cubicle or even a shop where the exits are unknown can be a terrifying prospect.

Where Does Anxiety Come From?

In this chapter we will help you acquire an understanding of what anxiety is. There is a lot of truth in the statement 'fear of the unknown', and so to lessen the fear and uncertainty associated with anxiety, we will share the basics so that we can put you in an informed position of power. You absolutely *can* get better, and understanding is a key component to start you on that journey.

The experience of anxiety can be very distressing. However, an important fact to acknowledge is that anxiety is entirely normal. The ability to create anxiety is something that has existed in humans since we were cavemen. It was an essential and often life-saving mechanism designed to protect us from dangers, such as ferocious wild animals. Simply put, it's our evolutionary survival tool.

> *When faced with potentially harmful or worrying triggers, feelings of anxiety are not only normal but necessary for survival.*

This human protection system is commonly known as the 'fight-or-flight' response, and sometimes referred to as 'fight, flight or freeze'.

To protect us from real dangers, the fight-or-flight response releases adrenaline. The adrenaline primes the body to fight for a short period, by creating a burst of energy.

Equally, adrenaline enables us to flee – with faster than usual reaction times and a speed we couldn't otherwise achieve or sustain. The reason this occurs is that the dose of adrenaline increases the heart rate, which pumps our oxygenated blood around the body faster. It also stimulates faster breathing, to increase oxygen levels in our bloodstream and provide our limbs with the extra energy necessary to fight or flee from danger.

The freeze response occurs before deciding to take flight. Most mammals freeze for a few milliseconds to assess the situation. Sometimes staying frozen in place, or playing dead, is the best defence. This freeze response has been highlighted in recent times, such as during the Bataclan shootings in Paris, by people who have utilised this element of our protection mechanism to survive a terror attack.

Anxiety in a Safe Situation

We now live in a world where we are safe from ferocious animals and it's rare to encounter actual physical danger. As a result, anxiety is being triggered by situations that are emotionally challenging but not life-threatening. The fight-or-flight response is often being inappropriately activated during normal, everyday situations when facing issues such as work, money, family life and health, which demand our attention without necessarily requiring the fight-or-flight reaction.

Symptoms of Anxiety

The symptoms of anxiety caused by the spike of our stress hormone, adrenaline, are varied and numerous, but most people will experience some of the following:

- **Increased heart rate or sense of heart palpitations**

- **Over-breathing (hyperventilating)**
- **Shaking**
- **Muscle tension**
- **Tension and tightness, or sense of compression, in the chest**
- **Feeling hot**
- **Feeling sweaty and clammy**
- **Heaviness or numbness in the arms and legs**
- **Tingling sensation in the arms and legs**
- **Numbness or tingling in the face**
- **Nausea**
- **Flatulence**
- **Need to use the toilet more often**
- **Headache**
- **Dry mouth**
- **Hypervigilance**
- **Hypersensitivity**
- **Light-headedness**

Reactions to Anxiety

For those who suffer from anxiety with an identifiable cause, although still unpleasant, there is an element of reassurance in knowing what the reason or trigger is. Certain actions can then be taken to alleviate the anxiety, such as avoidance, counselling, therapy, medication, distraction or relaxation techniques.

For those who are unaware of the cause or trigger, although the same solutions are available, the lack of a reason can magnify the situation and heighten the anxious feelings. We've worked with clients who said they felt like they were going mad, as they couldn't work out what was causing their anxiety.

Many people who suffer anxiety become insular and avoid social situations because they feel embarrassed or ashamed, and worry that perhaps they will faint, vomit or embarrass themselves. But there is nothing to be embarrassed about: although it can feel like a very isolated and lonely state, the statistics on anxiety will help you realise that you are far from being alone.

In 2013, there were 8.2 million cases of anxiety in the UK, and it's estimated that a further 13 per cent of the adult population will develop a specific form of anxiety known as a phobia at some point in their life.[1]

Equally alarming are statistics from the Anxiety and Depression Association of America, suggesting that 'anxiety disorders are the most common mental illness in the US, affecting 40 million adults'. It also states: 'Anxiety disorders are highly treatable, yet only 36.9 per cent of those suffering receive treatment.'[2]

Anxiety Disorders

Anxiety disorders occur when a reaction is out of proportion to what might normally be expected in a situation, and are often coupled with recurring exaggerated and intrusive thoughts or concerns.

According to the charity MIND, anxiety disorders can be classified into nine main types:

1 Generalised anxiety disorder (GAD) – a disorder involving excessive worry over non-specific life events, objects and situations.

2 Panic disorder – sudden attacks of intense terror and apprehension.

3 Phobias – irrational fear and avoidance of an object or situation.

4 Social anxiety disorder – fear of being negatively judged by others or publicly embarrassed.

5 Obsessive compulsive disorder (OCD) – compulsive behaviours, thoughts or actions that are repetitive, distressing and intrusive.

6 Post-traumatic stress disorder (PTSD) – anxiety from a previous trauma such as military combat, sexual assault, a hostage situation or a serious accident. PTSD often leads to flashbacks, and the sufferer may make behavioural changes to avoid triggers.

7 Health anxiety – obsessing about ill health, assuming any ache or pain is something serious, and researching symptoms and ailments.

8 Body Dysmorphic Disorder (BDD) – excessively obsessing and worrying about a specific body part or physical appearance, fearing and/or seeing an issue or imperfection others do not see.

9 Perinatal anxiety or perinatal OCD – an anxiety which develops during pregnancy or in the first year after giving birth.

NHS UK supports our belief that feelings of anxiety at certain times, and within context, are completely normal, and that medical help should be sought only if anxiety is negatively affecting your daily life or causing distress.

However, as we are stimulus-response animals, anything can potentially trigger a memory from our past or a schema that can lead to feelings of anxiety, without us being consciously aware of it – such as music playing subtly in the background, or even a smell.

A great example of this is a man we met some time ago who spoke about 'random' anxiety attacks. We explained our belief that anxiety is never random, and suggested he keep a notebook to document his anxiety episodes. He soon discovered a pattern: whenever someone patted his arm, he would feel sorrowful and anxious. We later discovered he was a young man when his father passed away. At the funeral, people would invariably pat him on the arm to offer their condolences, and this created a negative schema. Without realising it, a pat on the arm was triggering a negative emotional response in this man. This realisation alone gave him a sense of relief. However, we also conditioned his schema by helping him to appreciate that the pat on the arm was not the cause of his father's death, but rather a display of friendship, compassion, and people caring for him and his dad. Therefore, it should be looked at instead as a positive affirmation of his father's memory. He completely accepted this, and his anxiety stopped.

As we take you through every step of our advice, you will begin to understand what kind of anxiety you are experiencing. Once we've helped you identify your triggers – don't worry if you're not yet aware of them – we will be able to give you the techniques to help you through your anxiety.

A great place to start is for you to document your anxiety episodes. You can use your diary, a notebook or the Notes app on your mobile phone. This will really help you to establish possible patterns, causes and triggers of your anxiety, while also providing you with a positive distraction which can alleviate building anxiety.

Note down the following whenever you're feeling anxious:

- **Date**
- **Time**
- **Where am I?**
- **Who am I with?**
- **What can I see?**
- **What can I hear?**
- **What can I smell?**
- **What can I taste?**
- **What am I touching?**
- **What am I feeling?**
- **Why might I be feeling this?**
- **What was I thinking about?**

We have been where you are today – paralysed by anxiety – but by using our schema conditioning psychotherapy, you will achieve the mental repositioning and gain the tools to address the physical experience you are having now.

3

The Speakmans' Schema Conditioning Psychotherapy

When I met you both at the seminar in Manchester last January, I couldn't even sit in the room as my emetophobia [phobia of vomit] was so very extreme, and it controlled my whole life. After two treatment sessions I now feel that I can attempt anything and I am in control. I can't find the words to express how much you have changed my and my family's lives. You give hope to people, and show that there is light at the end of the tunnel, as nothing is forever and you can live and enjoy life. You listen and don't judge, and understand what people are going through, when many GPs sadly don't and therefore make you feel silly. I am so glad that I saw you both on ITV's This Morning, *for I wouldn't be where I am now otherwise.*

Clare

In this chapter, we will share the method and process that we use when working with clients suffering from anxiety, in the hope that you can start to remove your barriers, dilute your fears and positively change your perspective on painful memories. We want you to realise your potential and your positive future, free from the burdens of the past. Life is for living!

We believe that deep inside, everyone knows the person they would love to be, the life they would love to live, and that they deserve it. Yet happiness and emotional peace can seem unattainable, with numerous invisible barriers, negative thoughts, and various fears and anxieties preventing us from living that life.

How Does Our Therapy Work?

Many people comment after having observed our therapy and work – whether in person, at our workshops, on television, or via the films on our website and our YouTube channel – that the solution often appears to be simple. In fact, we frequently hear that 'surely it can't be that easy'. The truth is that most often it is! We hope that by reading the many successful case studies within this book, you will find personal references and similarities that will enable you to address your own challenges.

I attended the Birmingham workshop last Sunday. I'd like to share with you how I feel now. I came with what I thought was a severe blood pressure test/white coat syndrome phobia. I raised my hand when Nik asked if anyone was happy to talk about their phobia. While talking about my dad's high blood pressure and stroke, and how my palpitations begin in the doctor's waiting room, Eva cut in with: 'I don't think you have a blood pressure phobia, I think you're frightened of receiving bad news.' This was a light bulb moment for me. I have, over the last few years, had hypnotherapy, countless therapy sessions, acupuncture, meditation – you name it, I've tried it – for what I thought was general health anxiety/phobia. Over the last few days I've had time to really think about this, and I understand now what triggered this and that Eva's statement was 100 per cent accurate. I feel like a weight has been lifted and I can't thank you all enough.

Sarah

As you will see from the case studies we share, we usually manage to help people within only one therapy session. We have such a fast and positive impact because our clients complete a very detailed questionnaire (see page 16) prior to meeting us. From this, we are able to understand the potential life traumas and events that may have caused our clients' anxiety, and we can then prepare a personalised therapy session for them.

Conditioning Your Negative Schemas

We want to make addressing and changing your negative schemas simple. This amazing process of overcoming your issues should be as straightforward as possible, so that you can get on with the important job of making yourself happier, feeling more fulfilled and allowing your life to flow more easily.

However, there is work involved on your part. Once you have our formulas, suggestions and information, we pass the baton to you, asking you to use them to challenge your own life.

We remember buying our first iPhones and being amazed at how they saved us so much time by allowing us to access our emails on the go. Years on, our iPhones have become mobile computers and are present in almost every moment of our lives. We update them regularly, making sure they are running on the latest software and functioning at their best. How amazing would it be if everyone had that same determination to upgrade our own thought processes and beliefs, updating our behaviours in line with our changing lives?

Take a few moments now to consider how many of your behaviours are stopping you achieving things you want, and are therefore no longer needed in your life. They will be behaviours from older operating systems and ideas you had when you were younger. Just like your phone, it's time to upgrade your own operating systems – your schemas – to offer you the best possible life, free from unnecessary anxiety.

The Speakman Way

A schema allows us to organise and interpret information. It is a learned or copied pattern that becomes an automatic reference for how we think, act and ultimately behave. In our therapy, we help locate negative schemas which are a result of past negative life events. These may have evoked emotions such as fear, envy, embarrassment, grief or shame. Then we help to update and mentally reposition the memory of the event, thereby amending and upgrading its negative emotions to positive ones.

The therapy that we have developed over the last two decades is called 'schema conditioning psychotherapy' (not to be confused with 'schema therapy', a different type of therapy that we do not practise).

Schemas direct our behaviour

In 1952, psychologist Jean Piaget defined a schema as 'a cohesive, repeatable action sequence possessing component actions that are tightly interconnected and governed by a core meaning'. In simple terms, schemas are the basic building blocks of intelligent behaviour and a way of organising knowledge. You could also think of schemas as files containing vast amounts of information, which are stored within the filing cabinet of your memory. Each file tells us exactly how to react when we receive incoming stimuli. Schemas are 'learned references' that allow us to be proficient in everything we do – from brushing our teeth to driving our car, from how we communicate to how we react to a spider.

For example, we all have schemas for how having a meal in a restaurant should happen and what to expect. The schema will be a pattern that includes looking at the menu, choosing your food, ordering the food, eating it and paying the bill. Whenever you are in a restaurant, you will run this schema.

The blank canvas of new life

We are born a blank canvas – tabula rasa.

Every healthy, typical brain has the same lack of knowledge at birth. As we grow up, we learn from our parents, extended family, friends, peer groups and our own individual experiences of our surroundings. Our personal processing of the world completely dictates how we see ourselves and our environment, and how we behave and react to any event or situation that we are faced with.

We are all born with a small number of innate schemas. These are the cognitive structures underlying our reflexes. For example, babies have a sucking reflex that is triggered by something touching their lips, and a grasping reflex stimulated when something touches their hand.

Most schemas, however, are learned – as a result of copying the behaviour of our parents or people we're in close contact with, or through our own interpretation of personal life experiences.

Developing schema conditioning psychotherapy

Having trained in various fields of therapy over twenty years, we identified that we had great skill in helping people change their mindset and behaviours just by talking with them, encouraging them to look at situations from a different perspective.

We believe that people possess an inner wisdom, and we are able to tap into their understanding of why they think and behave the way they do. With this new understanding of self, as a result of our talking therapy, we can change their negative schemas. This is the foundation of our therapy and why we so passionately want to share with you the secret to overcoming anxiety. The good news is that the power to overcome your pain, right now, is within you.

There is a misconception that we use some kind of magic, hypnotherapy or confusion methods, but our therapy is no more than a straight-talking conversation.

A simple change in perspective

Your anxiety is driven by your negative schemas – but all schemas can be changed. Here's a simple example of how.

The British public are known for their love of talking about the weather, and most often we complain about the cold and rain. However, in the summer of 2018 the UK endured a heatwave. We experienced back-to-back days of scorching temperatures and sunshine; our lawns were brown, our plants were wilting, and we suffered sticky, sleepless nights. People started complaining about the heat as it had gone on for too long. We didn't want the heatwave to last – watching the country change felt unsettling, and when it started to rain we were joyous!

Changing your mind

Another example of how schemas can instantly change and be 'conditioned' is if you learned that a friend you care about and trust has stolen from you or spoken badly about you. This new information provides you with an alternative perspective, and your schema about that friend changes immediately. As a result, your behaviours and feelings towards them also change. Essentially this is how our therapy works: we help to change your perspective forever. Our skill is always being able to see an alternative perspective very quickly, and then effectively and precisely delivering it to the person we are helping.

These are the five steps we use to help change schemas and overcome anxiety. Follow them to address and alter your anxiety too.

1   Find the original event. Remember that you may have more than one anxiety-causing event, and that's perfectly normal. Just concentrate on one at a time.

2   Question how you interpreted the event. How old were you, and how did you perceive the event at that age? Consider how your perception then could be flawed or inaccurate, seeing it from an adult's perspective now.

3   Collate contrary evidence to positively condition your perception of the event and your resulting schema. If you find it difficult to challenge your current belief, ask a friend who you consider wise and positive. Explain you're

trying to improve your feelings by looking for a positive alternative perspective.

4 See the event for what it was and not how it felt. If you were a third party and this had not happened to you, how might you have seen it differently?

5 Decide to be a victor, not a victim. If things from your past continue to affect you then you are still a victim of that person or event. Make a decision today that you will be a victor of your past: you survived it and you are prepared to alter your perspective to set yourself free.

> *Our words and individual thoughts can have the power over any psychiatric medicine.*

4

The Speakmans and Anxiety

I used to have a phobia of all transport. It started off in a plane and then it went out into cars, trains, tubes – I couldn't go on any form of transport. It really debilitated my life to the point where I couldn't go out anymore. I never thought I would get over it, until I met the Speakmans. Nik and Eva changed my life from the day I went to see them. Now I can get in a car, on a tube, and go on holiday; it has opened my life up. If you think that you can't get over it and that they won't be able to help you, then think again because they will do everything in their power to help you.

Louise

How We See Anxiety

In this chapter we would like to share our experience with anxiety and anxiety disorders. Anxiety can seem scary, complicated and random, but when you understand it, you can take control of it.

We do not believe that anyone is born with, or genetically predisposed to, an anxiety disorder: if that were the case, we would not have been able to help thousands of people overcome their anxiety disorders through our therapy.

Some of these people knew exactly how their anxieties had originally manifested, yet many had no idea whatsoever, and some believed that because they had an anxious parent, grandparent or other close family member, their issue must be hereditary or 'genetic'.

The NHS states that the cause of generalised anxiety disorder (GAD) is not fully understood, and that it is likely a combination of several factors are involved, including:

* **Overactivity in areas of the brain involved in emotions and behaviour.**

* **An imbalance of the brain chemicals serotonin and noradrenaline, which are involved in the control and regulation of mood.**

* **The genes you inherit from your parents – you're estimated to be five times more likely to develop GAD if you have a close relative with the condition.**

* **Having a history of stressful or traumatic experiences, such as domestic violence, child abuse or bullying.**

* **Having a painful long-term health condition.**

* **Having a history of drug or alcohol misuse.**

The NHS also adds that many people develop GAD for no apparent reason.[3]

But our experience suggests that there is always a trigger for anxiety. Therefore, we do not agree that any anxiety disorder can be 'generalised', as we will discuss further in Chapter 5; nor have we ever worked with or met anyone who has suffered from anxiety for no apparent reason.

Chemical imbalance and genetics

Our view is that, if a chemical imbalance or genetics was a cause of anxiety, our therapy would be futile. Yet we have successfully treated people who have been told by medical professionals that their anxiety is as a result of these things.

It is generally accepted that blood tests, urine samples, scans and X-rays cannot indicate depression or an anxiety disorder: any diagnosis is opinion-based. This is a frightening thought – someone can be labelled and carry that label with all its repercussions for the rest of their life, merely from someone's opinion.

Schema – you become what you think about.

In *The Key to Upgrading Your Life* we highlighted the dangers of giving labels to people, and how we become what we think about. Would you just accept it if a doctor diagnosed you with cancer, hepatitis or any other disease only by speaking to you? No: you would want blood tests, scans – evidence. However, when it comes to mental health this is what happens all the time, often leading the sufferer to feel broken, incurable and hopeless, based on an opinion rather than facts.

It is biochemical processes that release so-called 'happiness hormones' such as serotonin, oxytocin, endorphins and dopamine. However, we can take responsibility to encourage and stimulate production of these hormones through laughter, exercise, nurturing our relationships and cultivating happier thoughts. Poor mental health is no different from poor physical health. We accept that healthy eating and exercise will improve our physical health, and the same applies for good mental health: we have to nourish ourselves, our thoughts and our environment.

We also believe that behaviours are learned, not genetically inherited. Just as we mimic the accent of our parents from birth, we also copy behaviours, including anxious behaviours. This is especially prevalent with phobias: around 40 per cent of the people we treat for arachnophobia have learned their fear from seeing a close family member scream when seeing a spider in childhood.

It is important to state that we are huge advocates of our National Health Service. Having observed countries where healthcare is only available to those who are insured or can afford to pay, we feel exceptionally grateful and valued for the free healthcare we are gifted in the UK. However, in relation to mental health, NHS resources are very stretched, and its approach is somewhat antiquated. The therapies on offer remain one-size-fits-all, with medication the go-to for most sufferers. Though it can be helpful in the short term, medication only masks the symptoms of anxiety, rather than fixing the original cause for the long term.

Future psychologists

The number of people being diagnosed with anxiety disorders is continually on the increase, yet the world of psychology appears to be looking for abnormalities of the brain and brain chemicals as opposed to solutions. This could be an explanation for why we are often ignored when we offer a solution, and hence why we choose to share our work through the media.

We don't believe what we see; we see what we already believe.

We have found that anxiety is a consequence of negative schemas and copied or learned behaviours.

What are the Causes of Your Anxiety?

What you are experiencing now is the result of the human evolutionary response of fight or flight to difficult situations or life experiences.

Our therapy is focused on looking for the schema that has stimulated this fight-or-flight response, and then cognitively restructuring or conditioning the memory to sever its link to the anxiety response.

Anxiety is a symptom, and there are two types of trigger or cause:

1 Learned behaviour – copying a parent, friend, family member, peer group, etc.

2 Learned response to a negative life event – trauma, bullying, bad parenting, abuse, accident, etc.

Our primary objective when helping someone is to find that trigger or cause, to help alleviate the associated symptoms.

- **Anxiety is triggered by a thought.**

- **The thought is created because of a schema.**

- **The schema is learned or created during a life event.**

- **Most anxiety-causing schemas are due to a trauma or negative event.**

Are we born fearful?

We are born with only two 'fears': a fear of loud noises and a fear of falling. You will notice that a baby flinches if a door slams, or a toddler instinctively puts their arms out to catch themselves if they fall.

While these fears are primarily a protection mechanism, they are not linked to our fight, flight or freeze mechanism unless a subsequent negative experience occurs, e.g. being involved in the aftermath of a bomb blast, or being pushed and falling on broken glass.

It is only when we are in a heightened state of fear or anxiety, and our brain is provided with evidence and justification that we need to be protected from something, that a phobia, irrational fear or anxiety may develop.

Although most schemas are positive and hugely helpful in life, it is the negative or negatively associated schemas that cause problems. If they are not dealt with and conditioned, they could last a lifetime, with devastating effects on the quality of your life and those around you.

We are essentially the sum of all our schemas, and the bad ones can have a negative impact on how we act and feel.

Events can affect people very differently, causing the creation of different schemas within people who experience the exact same situation. For example, Eva grew up in a house where alcohol was regularly abused, and there are members of Eva's family who created the schema that alcohol is a good way to unwind and deal with problems. Conversely, Eva's schema is: 'I have seen how destructive alcohol can be, so I would never drink often and certainly never to excess.'

What does this mean to me?

The reason for the vast differences in people's beliefs, actions and behaviours is fundamentally that, no matter what we observe, hear or experience, every minute of every day our individual minds are unconsciously asking the question, 'What does this mean to me?'

The answer to this question is entirely individual – the interpretation of every event we face is based on our existing schemas, and so too are the resulting response and behaviours.

How to Change Our Anxiety Levels

To be able to change your life for the better and feel less anxiety, you have to change your schemas.

You cannot control events around you, but you can control your choice of what to focus on, what things mean to you, and subsequently how to act or what to do. These three things ultimately shape our lives. You can bring control back to any situation when you change your focus.

> *The one thing we all have full control over is what we choose to focus on. We can focus on what's going wrong and feel bad, or we can choose to focus on what's going right and feel good.*

This is the most empowering part of our therapy, which we want you to grab with both hands and believe: if you want to change your life, then *you* have to change. If you want life to get better, then *you* have to get better. That's simply the only way it happens. You can overcome anxiety: the power is within you.

By understanding this, you can change old negative patterns, beliefs and behaviours in order to be the person you choose to be, without having to endure the internal conflict caused by wanting to behave a certain way yet being driven by conflicting negative schemas from the past.

Flicking the switch

Knowing that our brains are much the same when we're born means you can be like any other person on the planet you choose to be.

For instance, if you have a couple of relationships that go wrong you could end up believing that all relationships are bad. You may choose to stay single for years until you realise that actually, it wasn't being in a relationship that was bad, but being in a relationship with the wrong person. When that 'flick of the switch' happens in your head and you realise that incompatible partners rather than relationships were to blame, you will feel ready to move on, and it will be clear how wrong your old schema was.

You can condition your old schema in a split second with new evidence, and that new positive schema can set you free.

> *If you do what you've always done, you'll get what you've always got.*

Manage or cure?

A question we're often asked is: 'Can my anxiety disorder be cured, or will I just have to try and manage it for the rest of my life?'

An anxiety disorder is not a disease, so it is not a condition that needs to be 'cured', as such.

For us, an anxiety disorder is symptomatic behaviour that occurs because of a mismanagement of emotions. With the right help and direction, you can overcome an anxiety disorder successfully and permanently. Management of an anxiety disorder should only be a temporary requirement until you can change the negative schema.

In the next few chapters, we will show you how we have helped to condition and positively change people's schemas. By sharing the formulas we used, we hope you too will get the 'flick of the switch' you need to break those debilitating anxiety-inducing habits you've been carrying around with you – habits you no longer want – and new ways of thinking that will transform your life.

5

Generalised Anxiety Disorder

From a very young age, I felt like some sort of 'anxiety' was slowly taking over and it was affecting me in everything I did. I'd lose sleep over the thought of certain things and I wouldn't want to leave the house or talk to anyone. As I got older, I just came to terms with the fact that I'd never get rid of it, so the best thing to do was to just deal with it. I dealt with it by trying everything – basic therapy, medication, literally everything – and no one understood me when I tried explaining it. In fact, some people laughed, but that was the frustrating part as no one could get their head around why I felt like this sometimes. Most upsettingly, I didn't understand why I had it. That was until I met Nik and Eva. Straight away I felt this incredible energy from them, and they pinpointed exactly why I had this issue and made me feel like I wasn't the only one. As the session went on, I felt this weight slowly lifting off my shoulders as all those questions that I had battled with in my head since a young age were finally getting answered, quite simply too. I never believed in miracles until I met the Speakmans.

Jake

One of the most common forms of anxiety is generalised anxiety disorder. In this chapter, we will help you understand and recognise the symptoms of GAD, and show you how our schema conditioning psychotherapy can be useful even if you don't know when or why your anxiety levels have risen.

We are often approached about generalised anxiety disorder, particularly at our workshops, and it appears to be a more and more common diagnosis. People approach us, usually with the same solemn demeanour, saying, 'I have GAD and have been told I will probably have to live with it, as it doesn't have a starting point to work with.'

While the NHS states that 'many people develop GAD for no apparent reason', this has certainly not been our experience. If your doctor had time to sit with you and discuss the trials and tribulations of your life, they might be able to identify the triggers that cause your GAD. But with increasing demands on GPs' time, this is rarely a service they can offer; we want to share the techniques we have used to successfully treat thousands of clients with GAD, suggesting some solutions to ease your anxiety too.

What is GAD?

Generalised anxiety disorder (GAD) is a broad diagnosis that covers a host of symptoms. People diagnosed with GAD tend to suffer from anxiety most of the time, and most days. They worry about everything from health and finances to friends, relationships and daily tasks, and often think the worst will happen in every situation.

Symptoms of GAD include:

- **Worry**
- **Stress**
- **Insomnia**

- **Restlessness**
- **Irritability**
- **Tension**
- **Nausea**
- **Excessive tiredness**
- **Sense of dread**
- **Physical trembling**
- **Lack of concentration**
- **Muscle tension**
- **Headaches**
- **Sweating**

The anxiety felt by someone with GAD can interfere with their ability to function day to day, or even just to relax. The consequence of creating anxiety so frequently is exhaustion: the adrenal glands are in overdrive and the fight-or-flight response is overstimulated.

People with GAD may also have other anxiety disorders, such as obsessive compulsive disorder or a phobia, or they may suffer from, or are overcoming, addiction.

How GAD is Diagnosed

To be diagnosed with GAD, the patient must have three or more of the following six symptoms (with at least some symptoms having been present for more days than not for the past six months):

1 Restlessness or feeling keyed up or on edge.

2 Being easily fatigued.

3 Difficulty concentrating or mind going blank.

4 Irritability.

5 Muscle tension.

6 Sleep disturbance.

We believe that there is a reason for this anxiety, and when we work with clients who have been diagnosed with GAD, we always discover the original catalyst or cause.

How We See GAD

Unlike an anxiety disorder such as a phobia or PTSD where there is generally an obvious event from which it developed, we have found that numerous factors exist with GAD. For this reason, it is frequently the case that overcoming or reducing the effects of anxiety will require more than just challenging and positively conditioning past negative schemas. There are some practices to try, and environmental changes that you may have to make too.

We believe that positivity is learned, and that we are a product of our environment, just as our accent is.

Equally, there is no instruction manual for life. We are not taught how to deal with trauma, bereavement, negative environments or inefficient parents. We cope with negative issues using behaviours we have learned and personal interpretations of past life experiences to apply the best solution available to us, based on what we know.

In our therapy sessions we try to redress the balance of positive and negative input. Through conversation, we offer an alternative positive perspective on previous negative life events, to alleviate the burden of how they were originally perceived and to challenge the anxiety-inducing schemas that were established.

> ***Thoughts create feelings, and therefore changing our thoughts positively, changes our feelings positively too.***

Although we accept that there are conditions such as drug abuse, menopause and thyroid issues that can contribute to GAD, we do not accept that anxiety is ever 'general'. We believe there are always causes or triggers, found in one or all of the following:

* **Current life events – such as ill health or a bad relationship.**

* **Environment – such as our peer group, work, diet, sleep, finances and focus.**

* **Past life events – such as traumas and a turbulent childhood.**

* **Learned behaviour – such as having an anxious parent or carer.**

Overcoming GAD

It is important to understand that anxiety is a normal emotion in certain circumstances, and that we all face varying levels of anxiety throughout our lifetime.

However, the exercises and suggestions below aim to alleviate a general sense of anxiety and will help you to address its causes.

If you are struggling, speak with your doctor about arranging therapy to talk through your issues, which can offer you an alternative perspective on past events, as well as medication – should it be necessary – to lessen your symptoms in the short term. We believe anti-depressants, anti-psychotics and SSRIs should be considered only in emergency situations, until the root cause of the anxiety is found and resolved.

Dealing with triggers

Let's look at potential causes or triggers that you can address to help you positively condition negative anxiety-causing schemas.

CURRENT LIFE EVENTS

Your current life events will significantly affect your mood, so it's a good idea to note the things in your life that create negative feelings for you.

If there are elements of your life that impact you negatively, create a plan to make positive changes. Write down the things you feel you need to change, the steps you will take to change them, and start with one small step for each.

Be aware that there are likely to be certain situations you will be able to change, some you may not be able to change right now, and some you may never be able to change. For the situations you cannot change, or cannot change right now, you can work on changing your perception of them. A more positive perspective will help to improve your feelings.

> *Different actions create different results.*

ENVIRONMENT

You may not be able to change how people behave towards you entirely, but you do have control over your environment. Improving your environment can help to improve your mood and as a consequence your health too.

Studies suggest that we become like the five people we spend most time with: if you surround yourself with negative people, your conversation and mood will reflect that. Take a look at your social circle and endeavour to distance yourself from people who drag you down. Equally, spending more time with positive and fun friends will elevate your mood.

Your diet will also affect your mood. If you eat well, you will feel well; if you eat poorly, you will feel poorly. Keeping a food diary over a two-week period will give you a clear indication of what you need to reduce or increase. In general, reducing caffeine, sugar, gluten, dairy and saturated fats, and increasing fresh fruit, vegetables and oily fish will have a positive impact on your health and state of mind.

Staying hydrated by drinking lots of water is also a good way to improve your mental health and wellbeing. To keep your body working properly, you should drink a minimum of eight glasses of water each day.

Exercise will maintain a healthy body, but it also stimulates the production of hormones that elevate our mood. Joining a gym or aerobics class is a great opportunity to meet new friends too.

Good quality sleep is essential for a healthy mind and body. Insufficient sleep can have a detrimental effect on your mood, and sleep deprivation increases anxiety levels.

Take steps to aid a good night's sleep such as exercising, avoiding a heavy meal, alcohol or caffeinated drinks from the early evening, keeping your bedroom screen-free, meditating before bed, listening to relaxing music, and writing down any niggles that are occupying your mind – if you find yourself dwelling on them while trying to sleep, remind yourself that you have written them down so they will be waiting for you in the morning.

Finally, reduce physical mess and organise your space at home and work. A cluttered environment contributes to a cluttered mind, while a clean, orderly environment will help your mood.

PAST LIFE EVENTS

Negative or traumatic past events often have the biggest impact on our feelings of anxiety.

> *Do not let a painful past live on to create a painful future.*

For those suffering from GAD, there may be a number of past life events that need to be addressed.

Writing a timeline (see page 19) could help you to identify the events and memories that need to be conditioned positively. This can be done alone or with a therapist or positive close friend.

> *Sever the emotional links from the past by choosing to let go of guilt, anger, envy, hate and self-pity.*

Work through your timeline, one event at a time. Consider how each memory can be altered positively, even if only fractionally, so as to allow a new perspective.

LEARNED BEHAVIOUR

Your past does not have to equal your future.

Accepting that your anxiety is a learned behaviour is a positive first step. It can be helpful to remind yourself that the feelings of anxiety do not belong to you. When your fight-or-flight response is being stimulated, look around you and reassure yourself that there are no dangers. Then say: 'Thank you, but I don't need protecting right now.' This acknowledgement of your innate response will dilute your anxious feelings and behaviours.

CASE STUDY
Connor: Generalised Anxiety Disorder

With millions of fans worldwide and sellout arena tours, The Vamps had the world at their feet. But the band's bassist, Connor, suffered generalised anxiety disorder which included panic attacks and depression, preventing him from enjoying incredible moments others would give anything to experience.

Therapy and medication were not helping Connor, so he contacted us. Connor had become fearful of his anxious feelings and panic attacks, so first we wanted him to understand anxiety. We explained that anxiety is a message sent to protect you. But Connor had linked his protection mechanism to safe situations: our job was to find his triggers, and to break the link between normal daily experiences and his fight-or-flight response. Connor was neither fighting nor fleeing when his anxiety was triggered, because there was no real danger to face. This meant his built-up anxiety would overflow, creating a 'panic attack'. We asked Connor to think of these not as 'panic attacks' but 'protection attacks'.

Connor was desperate to feel better for an upcoming tour. He revealed that he felt fine about the UK leg, but was concerned about touring abroad. We needed to find the reason why Connor's fight-or-flight mechanism was being triggered, so we looked through his timeline together. In the negative column, two events stood out. Aged six, he had been in Thailand when he suffered an allergic reaction to nuts, leaving him unable to breathe. And on a family holiday to Greece aged nine, he had got stuck under a rock formation while swimming to a remote beach, again leaving him out of control and struggling to breathe.

We asked Connor how he felt now, as an adult, whenever he returned home to the UK after being abroad. As expected, he said he felt a great sense of relief and that he had reached his safe place. We were confident we had found the trigger to Connor's anxiety, which, due to its frequency, had been diagnosed as 'generalised anxiety disorder'. To us it was obvious that those two childhood episodes had created his anxiety.

Connor's schema – I struggle to breathe when I am abroad.

Connor now had his dream job, but his band's success meant his phone could ring at any time to tell him that a trip abroad was necessary, putting him on high alert every day.

However, after acknowledging that he had been to many countries with no further issues – always carrying his EpiPen and swimming only in safe environments – Connor accepted that he was not at risk. He became quite emotional having finally obtained an explanation for and relief from his constant anxiety, knowing that being abroad did not pose a danger to him. After our therapy, Connor has noticed a real difference in his day-to-day life and has since happily travelled on tour to several countries without anxiety.

6

Panic Disorder

This time last year I was having anxiety attacks, in an unhappy marriage and just not sure what I was doing. I'm now happily living by myself and taking on positive challenges like street dance and learning to play the piano. All of these things would have been impossible for me a year ago. I am so appreciative of your help. It was like a spa day for my brain and heart.

Lynsey

Most people will have experienced a panic attack in their lifetime. A panic attack feels like an anxiety overload, and is hugely unpleasant and often very frightening. Usually it is a one-off event that is over in a short space of time, having arisen from a shock or trauma. However, the frequency and severity of panic attacks can vary. For some, a single panic attack can be so bad that the fear of another occurring stops them in their tracks, and inhibits their life. For others, panic attacks appear to come from nowhere.

We have met a number of people with agoraphobia who have been unable to leave their home after a panic attack, for fear of experiencing another. Those who cannot explain their original panic attack often assume that going out was the cause; therefore home becomes a safe zone.

Schema – being away from home causes me to have panic attacks.

This is also common with driving phobias. Many people we have met have had what they perceive as an unexplained panic attack while driving. They then blame driving for the panic attack, linking their fight-or-flight response to the car. This creates feelings of anxiety every time they are in a car or try to drive and so they give up altogether, believing that they could pass out or have a panic attack while driving.

The fear of panic attacks is a significant problem for many. But in our experience, panic attacks are never random, and they can be overcome.

What is Panic Disorder?

Panic disorder first appeared in the *Diagnostic and Statistical Manual of Mental Disorders* in 1980.

A panic attack is an abrupt surge of intense fear or intense discomfort that reaches a peak within minutes.

To be diagnosed with panic disorder, four or more of the following symptoms have to occur:

- **Palpitations, pounding heart or accelerated heart rate**
- **Sweating**
- **Trembling**
- **Sensations of shortness of breath or smothering**

- **Feelings of choking**
- **Chest pain**
- **Nausea or abdominal distress**
- **Feeling dizzy, unsteady, light-headed or faint**
- **Chills or heat sensations**
- **Paresthesia (numbness or tingling)**
- **Derealisation, feelings of unreality or depersonalisation (detached from oneself)**
- **Fear of losing control**
- **Fear of dying**

Familiar Faces with Panic Disorder

Many people who suffer from panic disorder feel very alone, but this is certainly not the case.

EMMA STONE

Emma Stone recently told the *Wall Street Journal* that before getting involved in acting she suffered from intense panic attacks.

She said: 'The first time I had a panic attack I was sitting in my friend's house, and I thought the house was burning down. I called my mom and she brought me home, and for the next three years it just would not stop. I would go to the nurse at lunch most days and just wring my hands. I would ask my mom to tell me exactly how the day was going to be, then ask again thirty seconds later. I just needed to know that no one was going to die and nothing was going to change.'[4]

ELLIE GOULDING

Ellie Goulding needed therapy and medication to cope after suffering a panic attack where she thought she was going to die. She revealed she started getting anxious after bad relationships convinced her that she was fat with a big nose.

In a *Metro* article, Ellie said: 'One day after a shoot I was on a train going to a funeral and my heart was pounding; I thought I was having a heart attack. When I got to Cardiff, the next train was cancelled, so I had to get in a cab with strangers to Hereford. I was so scared I reached over to this woman and said, "I think I'm dying." I called a friend to take me to hospital, where they told me it was just a panic attack. From that day, I kept having them. It was the weirdest time of my life. Sick, horrible things would go through my mind but I didn't want to draw attention to myself . . . It got to the point when I couldn't even get into the car and go to the studio.'

Ellie learned through cognitive behavioural therapy (CBT) that she was being affected by negative events in her childhood, including her father walking out when she was five.[5]

JEMMA KIDD

In an interview with the *Daily Mail*, Jemma revealed that she had suffered from an anxiety disorder during her twenties.

She stated: 'The attacks felt like that split second before a car crash, when the adrenaline whooshes through your body and you think you are going to die. So from the outside, I might have looked sorted, but on the inside, I was thinking, "If only you knew." [. . .] The attacks are so random and debilitating that you become fearful of the fear that they bring. You start to anticipate them and find yourself doing anything to avoid them. I stopped driving on my own; I manipulated my life so that when I had to go somewhere,

I had someone with me. I couldn't go into the supermarket or anywhere crowded. If I was going to stay at someone's house for the weekend, I would be anxious for about ten days before and would insist on knowing how close they lived to a hospital. The symptoms were so real that I believed I could have a heart attack at any time.'[6]

How We See Panic Disorder

We are constantly asked for advice on how to deal with panic attacks.

Panic attacks can appear to emerge out of nowhere, but there are always one or more triggers. These triggers can be something you see, hear, smell, touch, taste, feel or think about that has been linked to your body's fight-or-flight mechanism during a previous negative experience. But you are not in danger now: you do not need and cannot use the flood of adrenaline released, so the adrenaline overload causes a panic attack.

In the absence of an obvious trigger for the attack, an expectation arises that a further panic attack could occur at any moment, thus starting a cycle of anxiety and fight-or-flight response linked to the possibility of another panic attack, or to the location where the panic attack occurred or the activity you were engaged in.

Finding the Cause of Your Panic Attacks

A panic attack is a protective response. But if you are having a panic attack, you have linked your fight-or-flight mechanism to the wrong thing: a perceived danger, not a real danger. If you are unsure what has triggered this, you need to look for clues:

* Consider your first panic attack. Where were you and what was happening around you? What was going on in your life at that time? Write down every detail of that moment.

* Keep a diary of when you have a panic attack or feel your anxiety levels rising. Note where you are, what you can see, hear, smell, touch and taste. What are you thinking about? Do any of your answers have ties to a past anxious, upsetting or traumatic event?

* Consider whether you have had any previous negative experiences in that location or a similar location. For example, you may have had a panic attack in a supermarket, and walking into another supermarket triggers your fight-or-flight response.

* Complete a timeline of traumatic life events. For example: age three – bitten by a dog; age four – parents leaving me on my first day of school; age ten – losing my grandmother; age fifteen – being bullied; age nineteen – having my heart broken; age twenty-five – car accident; age thirty-six – made redundant from work.

* When you reflect on these negative life events, do they create any negative emotions today? Are there any links to the circumstances of your original panic attack? If so, these need to be challenged and changed positively.

* Try to pinpoint any schemas created in those negative events. For example, if you were bullied, your schema might be 'I'm not good enough', or if you had a car accident at a petrol station, you might have created the schema 'I am vulnerable at petrol stations.'

* Challenge your schemas. If you created them in childhood, consider their accuracy. Children often inflate situations or completely misinterpret them. If you created them as an adult, how could your summary of the original event be altered? How could it be perceived as less personal, less emotional, less frightening? For example: 'What are the chances of that happening again?' 'I may have felt in danger but I survived.' 'I would act differently now I'm older and wiser, so the event would have an entirely different outcome now.'

Steps to Manage Your Panic Attacks

* Panic attacks are a symptom: locating their causes and addressing them through altering your perspective to sever the link to your fight-or-flight response will relieve them.

* Appreciate your body's internal protection mechanism. Change your perspective to change your feelings: thank it for trying to protect you.

* Change your terminology. Words have a huge impact on how we feel. 'Panic attack' is a negative and emotive term that suggests you are out of control. Call it a 'protection attack™' instead: your body is in control and trying to help you.

* Take a look around and ask yourself: 'Where is the danger and what danger am I in right now?' Once you realise that there is no danger, reassure yourself: you have had a protection attack™ before and you survived, so you will survive this one too.

* Physically turn your negative feelings in the opposite
  direction. When you have a protection attack™, negative
  feelings will usually emanate from your stomach and
  come up to your mouth. Trace the feelings with your
  hands until you get the rhythm and can match the speed,
  then turn the feelings in the opposite direction and slow
  them down. This will give you control of your feelings and
  help to reduce them.

* Stop everything. Don't add to your adrenaline overload
  by rushing to find an escape. Instead, find a place nearby
  to sit down and gather your thoughts. Concentrate on
  steadying your breathing, and imagine that everything
  around you has gone into slow motion, including you.
  Find composure first, and then calmly leave if necessary.

* Focus on small goals. Distract your mind with simple
  steps to lessen your anxiety. For example, concentrate
  first on sitting comfortably, then identify which exit you
  will leave by, followed by what you would like for dinner
  or what you'll watch on TV that evening. Considering
  normal, calm activities will take you away from the panic.

* Laughter is at the other end of the happiness scale
  to fear, panic and anxiety (see page 7). When you first
  begin to feel the onset of a panic attack, immediately
  look for memories and images of a time when you
  laughed uncontrollably. This will also help to distract
  your mind.

* Chat! Once panic sets in, many sufferers feel isolated
  and embarrassed by their condition, and prefer to suffer
  alone. But one thing you can do to alleviate anxiety is to
  force yourself to socialise in a tense situation. Smile and
  seek out conversation. It may be hard at first, but you'll

find that occupying yourself is much easier than worrying about the onset of panicky thoughts.

CASE STUDY
Marion: Panic Attacks/PTSD

Marion could no longer work, be a passenger in a car, or travel. With her son Paul's wedding in Turkey approaching, her three children were desperate for help and brought her to our home. What should have been a two-hour journey took almost five hours due to Marion's panic attacks: they had to stop the car over twenty times to allow her to get out and walk around.

When they eventually made it, Marion's children begged us to help them get their mum back. They said that she had once been fun and carefree but had changed since her sister's murder. What had started as a panic attack in an elevator had now spiralled out of control.

We asked what had been happening in Marion's life when her first panic attack had occurred. Marion told us how her mood changed dramatically after hearing the in-depth details of her sister Pamela's death in court. Pamela had been dating a man she met online when she disappeared. Tragically, two months later, Pamela's body was found on the Yorkshire Moors; her boyfriend was convicted.

Although Marion was aware that she had PTSD, she could not understand why she had developed panic disorder. Her frequent panic attacks did not have an obvious cause.

We noticed that, as Marion relayed the details of her sister's murder, she became particularly distressed when she said that Pamela had been tied up in the back of her boyfriend's car and placed in a shallow grave. We asked

Marion to describe how she saw those events. Was she observing them, or was she seeing them through her sister's eyes? As we expected, she pictured the events as the victim: Marion would imagine herself tied up in the back of the car, and then being buried.

It was apparent from a log of Marion's panic attacks that they occurred whenever she saw or experienced anything linked to Pamela's murder, including cars, enclosed spaces and fields. Her attacks were being triggered by everything she envisaged in her own re-enacted version of what had happened.

Next, we asked Marion why she had made herself the victim. She said she hadn't realised this. We also pointed out that she was concentrating on her sister's death and forgetting to appreciate her life. Again, she said she hadn't known this was what she had been doing. Furthermore, we established that Marion had imagined Pamela still being alive in the boot of the car and the shallow grave, but her son confirmed that she was already dead before her body was placed in the car.

It was evident that Marion had created claustrophobia and anxiety triggers from her own imagined version of events, focusing on cars, the moors and enclosed spaces. But when we suggested that these were not to blame, Marion agreed she had got it wrong: these triggers were not responsible for the crime, and her version of events was not accurate.

We asked Marion if it was now time to celebrate her sister's life and remember her as she was: a lady full of life, fun, laughter and energy. The change in Marion was immediate: she beamed and said yes. We were thrilled to receive wedding photographs from Marion, showing her standing by her son's side on the beach in Turkey with a beautiful smile.

CASE STUDY
Alison: Panic Attacks/Social Anxiety

Alison's world was shrinking each day. She said that she had never been confident, but her feelings of extreme anxiety and panic attacks were starting to keep her shut away from the world. She could function, but she lived in panic until she could get home and lock her door.

Alison didn't socialise; her colleagues no longer invited her to functions as she had declined so many times, and she had lied to her mother about winning a spa retreat to avoid having to attend their family Christmas gathering for the first time. It was at this point Alison knew that she needed to take action.

When we met Alison, she was timid and fearful, displaying symptoms of a panic attack. After calming her down, we explained that when she said she had 'never' been confident, she had actually learned to lack confidence, probably due to a childhood event.

Talking with Alison revealed that her panic attacks were most prevalent when she was around people. She assumed she would do something to humiliate herself, and this would cause feelings of panic. We wanted to know why she had this belief.

Alison's schema – I will humiliate myself if I am around people.

We looked at Alison's timeline – most of her negative life events were her having a panic attack, telling us we needed to go further back in time to find the original event that had created her schema. We asked her to think back to a time, perhaps at school, when there were lots of people present and she felt humiliated. Suddenly her physiology changed. She became tense and said there was a day in junior school when she had been for a dental appointment and was late to class. As she walked in, the teacher said, 'Thank you for joining us – did you fancy a lie-in this morning?' The whole class roared with laughter; Alison blushed, and then there was more laughter as she was called a beetroot.

Watching Alison's discomfort merely recalling the story, and establishing that prior to this she did not remember being shy, we knew it had to be the originating event.

Next we asked Alison who had caused that feeling of embarrassment. First she said it was the class, but then corrected herself: 'Well, actually the teacher.' Then we asked if, given the opportunity to distract the class from a boring lesson with laughter, she would have done the same. Alison said, 'Yes, probably.' We asked if she would have laughed out of malice at the child walking in. She said no. We asked whether there might have been a similar scenario in her school career where Alison herself had laughed at another child. She said, 'Definitely.' Could Alison recall the children she had laughed at? Did she think badly of them now, or would she expect them to humiliate themselves if she saw them again?

Alison paused and said, 'I have never looked at it like this before. Of course not – I don't even remember anyone specifically, even though I know I did laugh at others in class.'

Alison's schema was now being positively conditioned.

We then asked Alison to consider the role of a teacher, and she confirmed that it is their duty to positively develop a child, rather than to break and humiliate them. In the circumstances, then, it was Alison's teacher who should feel embarrassed, knowing the negative effect that his inappropriate behaviour had on her.

With that, Alison sighed and we saw a huge release. Over the following months she shared with us her many achievements, including embarking on an evening college course, attending a colleague's baby shower, and successfully applying for a promotion at work.

7

Phobias

The Speakmans cured me of my phobia of dolls. I'm now not scared in the slightest; beforehand I was absolutely terrified. From working with Nik and Eva, I am now able to go into a shop, any shop, whereas beforehand, I could not go to Toys 'R' Us and would worry about what toys my daughter and niece would bring home. I am now happy to play with their toys with them. Christmas used to be a nightmare for me, as I would go in knowing I would be frightened, whereas now it does not faze me.

Stacey

In this chapter we will share our understanding and experience of phobias so that you can apply our formula to your own anxiety-causing fears and phobias.

We are probably best known for our success in treating phobias. No one is immune to them: they are the biggest contributor to feeling anxious.

When we started to appear on live television, working with phobias was a fast and very visual way to show how quickly a person can overcome a phobia or extreme anxiety. Testing a phobia before and after treatment while a client is wearing a heart monitor can deliver clear and powerful results.

Anxiety Live

On the UK daytime TV show *This Morning*, we have often met phobia sufferers live on air. We learn about their history of anxiety, and then the sufferer is attached to a heart monitor and shown a number of items in order to measure their phobic response. Having established their heart rate, we treat them backstage for an hour before repeating the original test live.

At the time of writing, we have successfully treated ninety-four phobias on live TV, including water, frogs, snakes, spiders, mice, small spaces, heights, dentists, clowns, masks, pantomime horses and even Simon Cowell!

Phobias are a fascinating topic for us and our phobia-free viewers, and our television work has helped other phobia sufferers to accept that they are not alone, that there is hope, and that they too can get better.

Do You Have a Phobia?

The NHS suggests that phobias are the most common type of anxiety disorder, estimating that around 10 million people in the UK have a phobia. The National Institute of Mental Health in America states that phobias affect around 19.2 million US adults.

Our belief is that if one person can have a phobia, then anyone can have a phobia, and that these figures are drastically underestimated. With that in mind, we conducted our own survey over a period of six months to ascertain how many people we came into contact with had a phobia.

We discovered that there were many who had a phobia but didn't realise it, mainly due to their terminology.

When a person has a phobia, they will often shape their lives to avoid what they consider to be dangerous.

A great example of this was our hairdresser, Charlotte. On a visit during our covert phobia survey, we asked her how she would feel if she were to see a spider walk across the salon floor, to which she replied, 'I would scream.' In that moment, we had discovered Charlotte's fear word was 'scream', and so we went on to ask her if anything else made her scream. She replied, 'Cows! I hate cows!' She explained that she would always ask her boyfriend to drive when they were in the countryside, and would cover her head if they passed a field with cows. We asked if there was anything else that would make her scream. Without hesitation, she said, 'Rats! I saw one near my car two weeks ago, where I always park for work. I had to run back to the salon and ask another stylist to move my car, and I haven't been able to park there since.' When we left the salon a couple of hours later, Nik said, 'Oh, Charlotte, can I ask you – do you have any phobias?' Charlotte said, 'No.'

This highlighted to us that potentially more people have phobias and phobic responses than we initially thought, but because of the terminology they use they do not consider themselves to have a phobia, and so life is easier for them. Because Charlotte didn't consider herself as someone with phobias, she was generally a laid-back, happy-go-lucky young lady. A fear of spiders, cows and rats did not dominate Charlotte's life, but unconsciously she would adapt her behaviour to accommodate the things that made her 'scream'.

What is a Phobia?

A phobia is medically classified as a type of anxiety disorder that causes an individual to experience extreme, irrational fear of or aversion to an object, situation, living creature or place.

Simple phobias

Simple phobias, sometimes referred to as 'specific' phobias, produce intense fear of an object or situation that is, in reality, completely or relatively safe. The phobic response is a reaction triggered by a single stimulus. Examples include:

- **Acrophobia – fear of heights**
- **Arachnophobia – fear of spiders**
- **Aquaphobia – fear of water**
- **Ophidiophobia – fear of snakes**
- **Claustrophobia – fear of enclosed spaces**

Complex phobias

Complex phobias are generally more challenging. They tend to include more triggers, as well as adaptive behaviours to cope with the phobia. Examples include:

EMETOPHOBIA

Emetophobia is a fear of vomiting, which can manifest as an avoidance of anything that could potentially lead to a sickness bug or vomit, including hospitals, schools, workplaces, restaurants or pubs, and certain foods such as chicken or fish. This phobia can also create an obsessive compulsive disorder (see Chapter 11) involving washing and cleaning, and can lead to agoraphobia (see below).

SOCIAL ANXIETY

Social anxiety is a fear of being judged negatively by other people. People with social anxiety experience feelings of inadequacy, inferiority, self-consciousness, embarrassment and humiliation, which can lead to self-harm, depression or loneliness, and agoraphobia.

AGORAPHOBIA

Agoraphobia usually develops from another fear or phobia that creates a belief that only the home is a safe zone, as the environment and events within the home can be relatively controlled. Agoraphobia can also be a consequence of post-traumatic stress disorder, where the outside world feels like a threat following a significant trauma.

Is it real in the world, or just to me?

A phobia is a flawed protection response. When someone has a phobia, they have created an inaccurate schema about an object, situation, living creature or place, and commanded their unconscious mind to protect them from what they perceive as a danger.

But the danger only feels real to the sufferer; it is not a real danger in the world. Hence it is considered irrational.

We have found that the longer someone has had a phobia, the bigger it appears to grow, and the more triggers are added. This is because when a phobia is triggered, other things are added to the 'avoid' list. For example, someone with a fear of heights is stuck in traffic on a high bridge. As they look down and notice they are high up, their protection mechanism kicks in, and suddenly bridges and driving are now to be avoided. This can make the sufferer's world become smaller and smaller over time.

Furthermore, just as a muscle will grow the more it is used, a phobia can do the same. For example, two children create a phobia on the same day – one starts to fear sharks after watching the film *Jaws*, while the other develops a fear of enclosed spaces when his sibling locks him in a cupboard as a prank. The claustrophobia will be triggered more often over time, and therefore is likely to be more severe: the sufferer will have to face more situations from which they will need 'protecting', such as elevators and toilet cubicles. Conversely, the shark phobia will be triggered far less frequently, and so the sufferer will not feel the need to be on high alert as often (unless they happen to live by the ocean).

Why do I always see what I am looking to avoid?

It is ironic that we seem to see the thing we're trying to avoid before anyone else. For example, people who have a fear of spiders will always be the first to spot one in a room. There are two reasons for this.

Every time our phobia is triggered, we add a note of our surroundings to the negative schema, meaning all new situations are compared to this. If there are any similarities, we will become hypervigilant because our internal protection mechanism releases adrenaline, dilating our pupils to allow more information into the eye.

The second reason is that people with a phobia are constantly scanning, without realising, for the thing they need to avoid in an effort to protect themselves. They live as a victim of the thing they are avoiding. This can become exhausting – a phobia is like a computer programme which is running constantly because of our heightened state of alert. Even at night, when we're trying to sleep, the programme never shuts down fully. Everyone we've helped overcome a phobia has commented that they now get the best night's sleep they've had in years, and this is because the programme has finally been closed.

How Phobias are Created

Phobias can be debilitating – crippling, embarrassing and distressing. However, the good news is that no one is born with a phobia.

The simple answer as to how phobias are created is trauma.

You will no doubt have observed children's wonderfully animated and dramatic interpretations of everyday situations. If you ask a child to tell you about an event they found funny, often they giggle so much that they can barely get their words out. Equally, if you ask them to tell you about something scary they will describe it in the most exaggerated way possible. This high-stakes view of the world is what allows children to immerse themselves in magical fantasies, but a child's perspective on an experience is also often the culprit when anxiety and phobias are created.

There are two ways of acquiring a phobia:

1 Copying behaviour – e.g. witnessing a parent screaming at a spider. This is traumatic for a child. To children, grown-ups are protectors who teach them how to survive.

To see their parent fearful of a spider creates a schema linking the fight-or-flight response to the spider.

2 Experiencing a trauma – seeing, hearing or feeling something frightening causes a heightened state of negative emotion, and stimulates the protection mechanism. There is no time to calmly evaluate the situation; our memory of what occurred is often distorted.

No matter what we face, our unconscious mind is always asking the question: 'What does this mean to me?' Our response is based on the information we receive via our schemas, which have been created from our life experiences. This information feedback then dictates our behaviour. Therefore, if we experience a trauma or copy a behaviour as a child, we can only evaluate it from a child's perspective, with a child's limited life experience. This is why, even though as an adult you might know your phobia is ridiculous, you can't help behaving like the child that created the phobic protection schema – unless it is conditioned and the original event upgraded to be seen from an adult's perspective.

The Hidden Phobia

Many people we meet come to see us about one particular phobia, yet in therapy it transpires there is another underlying phobia that is causing the secondary phobia.

A good example is a lady called Ursula, who asked for our help overcoming her claustrophobia. She was certain that it started when she visited her brother in Australia and they went to a rooftop restaurant. They had to go up in an glass elevator, which she had no problem with initially. However, as she got higher she began to feel more and more unsafe.

She said from that moment on, she was unable to go in an elevator again.

We always pay attention to our clients' terminology and observe their body language, as these often provide us with clues. We noticed that Ursula would put her hands to her throat when she talked about trying to enter an elevator. This led us to ask whether she had ever felt she was unable to breathe. She said she could no longer wear anything around her neck, such as scarves or polo-neck jumpers, as she felt she was being suffocated.

We eventually located the origin of Ursula's fears, which were instilled when she fell into a fast-flowing stream on holiday and couldn't get out. As the water went over her head, she thought she was going to drown, until she was saved by a canoeist.

So, Ursula's underlying phobia was of suffocating, which led her to feel distressed in small spaces. Once we conditioned her perception of the 'drowning' event, her claustrophobia disappeared too.

Ursula was one of the most sceptical people we have helped, so her surprise at how calm she felt when we guided her into an elevator was incredibly rewarding.

> *Whether you say you can or you can't, you will always be right.*

This means if you tell yourself you can't then you won't be able to, whereas if you say you can then you will find a way.

Many people we see are unwittingly giving themselves the command *not* to find the origin of their phobia, as they consistently tell themselves: 'I don't know how my phobia started.'

If you tell yourself you don't know something, the door slams shut: the information will not present itself. It is far more beneficial to use language such as, 'I am unsure of the origin of my phobia, but I know that I know it and I know it will come to me.' This will encourage the information and relevant memories to come forward.

Overcoming a Phobia

The great news is that whatever your phobia is, you can overcome it. It is vital to address and alter your perception of the events that created your phobia. Start by asking yourself if the thing you are phobic of has actually done anything to you. Did it target you? Did it create a master plan specifically to traumatise you?

Once you change your perception of the thing in question, you will change how you feel. For example, if a dog once bit you, then the dog must have been scared; or perhaps the owner beat the dog and made it a nervous animal. Either way, the dog is not to blame. Even if you still struggle not to blame the dog that bit you, there is no reason to blame all dogs.

Here are some more examples of how you could alter your perception of something you are phobic of. Apply these approaches to whatever it is you fear:

* **If you were stuck in a broken elevator, then consider that because you got out, you were not trapped, just inconvenienced.**

* **If you saw your mother scream at a spider, it was your mother that scared you. The spider did nothing.**

* If a sibling chased you with a toy snake, it was your sibling that made you scared, not the snake. And of course, it was a toy, not a real snake.

* If you saw someone vomit because they overindulged in alcohol, it was their fault for drinking too much, not vomit's fault. Also consider being grateful to vomiting, as it stops people from being poisoned and therefore saves lives.

* If you once had a bad experience with a dentist, don't blame all dentists; just don't return to the one that upset you. That would be like going to a hairdresser, not being happy with the haircut, and then never getting your hair cut again as you blame all hairdressers.

* If you had a bad experience with being up high, ask yourself what the height did. How did it orchestrate that negative event? Why blame it when it simply exists and has no interest in you?

* If you have a fear of flying, consider what an aeroplane has ever done to you, except take you somewhere safely. How is an aeroplane to blame for turbulence? No more so than a car is to blame for a bumpy road.

If you can vindicate the thing you are phobic of, and find evidence to positively support it, you can overcome your fear.

Here are some further exercises to assist you in addressing your phobia:

WRITE IT DOWN

Ask yourself:

- **What exactly do I fear?**
- **What do I believe will happen?**
- **What am I protecting myself from?**
- **Why do I need to be protected from it?**

LOCATE THE ORIGIN OF YOUR PHOBIA

Ask yourself:

- **How might my phobia have started?**
- **What did I experience?**
- **What did I see?**
- **Did I watch something in a movie?**
- **Was my parent or a family member fearful?**
- **Did I see someone else react to the thing I am afraid of, or did I have a bad experience personally?**

FIND NEW EVIDENCE

If you know the origin of your phobia, write the event down.

* **Note how you may have got the facts wrong, or misunderstood the event. Were you a child when you created your phobia? If so, consider whether you would take a child's advice in adulthood. If not, why not?**

* Consider how the thing you are phobic of is to blame. Was it involved in orchestrating the event? If you have claustrophobia because a sibling locked you in a cupboard, how was the enclosed space to blame? Was it responsible for the trauma, or was your sibling?

* If you copied fearful behaviour, accept that the behaviour did not belong to you – so what right do you have to take on the same behaviour? Was the person you copied always right about other things? Did their phobia enhance or inhibit their life? If it inhibited their life, why would you want to copy it?

* Write down some positives about the thing you are phobic of. If you have a fear of flying, focus on how aeroplanes enable you to see the world and make beautiful lifelong memories.

* Finally, imagine you are a lawyer and you have to prepare a defence for the thing you are phobic of. How would you prove it not guilty of purposefully or maliciously causing harm?

If you do not know the origin of your phobia, repeat to yourself: 'I know I am unsure how my phobia started, but if I did know, what might it be?' This question is very helpful to remove mental blocks, and if repeated daily, it should enable the answer to surface.

Habit

If you have had a fear for many years, you may have created behavioural habits around it. For example, if you have a phobia of spiders, you may have created a habit of checking the corners of every room you enter.

While these habits usually stop as soon as the phobia has been successfully challenged and altered, some may remain. If they do, actively question them. For example, remind yourself that you no longer believe spiders are dangerous, so you no longer need to check the room. This should make the habitual behaviour disappear very quickly.

Positive intent

Some people give up on overcoming their phobia, claiming that it is very stubborn or 'deep rooted', or that they have tried everything. If these excuses resonate with you, it is important to consider and challenge any positive intent you may have for keeping the phobia.

For example, if the phobia gives you meaning in life, if it has become your identity, or if it was copied from a parent and you feel it gives you a connection to them, then you may be reluctant to let it go.

While a positive intent to retain a phobia exists, you are less likely to be open to counter evidence that will allow you to let it go. If this is the case, write down a list of how your life will improve without the phobia. Note your special qualities so you are not reliant on the phobia for your identity. Ask how others feel about you having a phobia – you may be surprised to learn that it upsets or irritates those around you.

For most sufferers, positive intent is not relevant, but it can exist and could be the roadblock in your journey to recovery, so it's worth considering.

Many people over the years have told us that simply by watching us deliver our therapy to a phobia sufferer on television, they have applied our words to their own situation and overcome their phobia. With that in mind, we will share some case studies and tips below so you can see the questions, considerations and formulas we use to change people's inaccurate phobic protection schemas, which we hope will assist you too.

CASE STUDY
Sarah: Dentophobia (Fear of the Dentist)

Most people do not particularly enjoy a trip to the dentist. But for Sarah, it was out of the question.

Sarah's phobia was so severe that she had spent her life eating sweets in the hope that she could rot her teeth and make them fall out. Shockingly, she had even tried to pull out her own teeth. She was in constant pain, her teeth needed urgent attention, and she was embarrassed at how bad they looked. She had given up her singing career, always spoke with her hand covering her mouth, wouldn't kiss her husband, and refused to be photographed.

Aged thirteen, trying to alert a new dentist that she was in discomfort, she was callously chastised, leaving her traumatised. From that day Sarah refused to return. Even the thought of going to a dental surgery made her chest tighten, her throat close up, and she would start to shake with anxiety.

During therapy, we took Sarah back to the event that had instilled her phobia. We then showed her some dental instruments. Looking at them, she told us that her anxiety was an eight out of ten. We explained to Sarah that her dentist's behaviour when she was a child was entirely wrong. He had told her to raise her hand if something hurt, yet despite following his instructions and raising her hand time after time, he completely ignored her and then became cross with her, resulting in her giving up and squirming in pain, then running out of the surgery door.

This one bad experience led Sarah to blame all dentists. But we explained to her that she should have blamed the perpetrator, not the profession. She admitted that she had seen a lot of good dentists prior to the trauma, yet she had been stuck in that moment with that one dentist ever since. We asked Sarah if she agreed that the only time she should be fearful was if she were to visit the same dentist who had caused her the trauma. She said, 'Yes, but to be honest, he's probably retired now as he was very old, so I'm never likely to see him again.' This was a huge realisation, and it was clear from her facial expression and body language that she was over her phobia.

Now we had to prove to Sarah that her schema had been successfully conditioned. We showed her the dental instruments again, and she started to laugh as she said that she would normally be 'freaking out'. She explained that she felt her heart should be racing, yet it wasn't.

After the session we took her to our local dentist, and for the first time in almost two decades she did not panic or run away. There and then he gave Sarah a full check-up, and she was the perfect, calm patient. The following week, Sarah had some much-needed work done on her teeth, which gave her a smile to be proud of, and so much more confidence.

Sarah later said that looking back at the person she was before therapy was like looking at a different person, and that her fear seemed so irrational now. The last time we spoke she was about to start her own business, which required lots of face-to-face meetings and, of course, lots of smiling.

CASE STUDY
Dawn: Ophidiophobia (Fear of Snakes)

Dawn had a phobia of snakes that started after watching a horror film called *Venom*, aged seven. Everything about snakes terrified her: seeing photographs, hearing people talk about them, and even the word 'snake'! She constantly checked her bed, her cupboards, her shoes and her toilet for snakes. She struggled to write the word and couldn't even look at plastic snakes. For her fortieth birthday, Dawn booked a dream holiday to Florida. However, she started to feel anxious about going in case she encountered any snakes.

Ophidiophobia is one of the most common phobias in the world, and so we agreed to try and cure Dawn live on air within a ten-minute slot.

We started by pointing out that there were five of us on the studio sofas: Dawn, two presenters and us. Yet only one person was fearful of snakes. We asked Dawn who had got it right about snakes, and who had got it wrong. Dawn replied that she had got it wrong.

Next we suggested that snakes were entirely disinterested in Dawn, yet it was she who kept seeking them out. Dawn agreed, having not considered the irony of her actions.

Then we told Dawn that when she watched *Venom*, she had created a behavioural schema relating to snakes based on the film's storyline, which was fictional. This was no different from watching the film *Garfield* and believing that cats can talk.

We explained that the reason Dawn acted irrationally was that she was consulting a seven-year-old child on how to react when she saw a snake. We asked if she would consult her own seven-year-old daughter about how to behave as an adult, and she replied: 'Never!'

Then we asked Dawn if she had any pets. She said she had a cat that would occasionally scratch her, so we asked if she was scared of her cat. She said no. We put it to Dawn that her cat had physically injured her, but no snake had ever done anything to her, and she started to question her inaccurate belief about snakes.

We asked whether it was fair to blame a snake when none had ever hurt her. She said no. We asked if she would reprimand a dog for never hurting her. Again: no.

We moved on to check what the age restriction had been for *Venom*. Dawn said it was probably an eighteen, and realised that she had been far too young to watch it – the purpose of the film was to scare, so it had achieved exactly what it set out to do. It was the film that had scared Dawn, not the snakes.

Finally, we explained to Dawn that she had spent almost thirty years in fear of something that had never harmed her, and she had victimised snakes for no reason at all. Dawn took this on board and accepted she had made an error. We showed her a picture of a snake, so that she could see it through the eyes of an adult for the first time.

A few moments later we brought in a real snake in a box and set it in front of Dawn. Although nervous, she was able to look at it, again something that was completely new for her. She then observed someone with a snake wrapped around them and admitted that previously she would have run away. By the end of the show, Dawn was able to hold a snake herself, without any fear.

CASE STUDY
Jane: Pediophobia (Fear of Dolls)

Doll phobias are relatively common, but for Jane it was causing her extreme anxiety on a daily basis. She could not allow her young daughter to have dolls in the home, and customers at the restaurant where she worked were asked to leave their children's dolls in their cars so as not to upset her.

Jane had sought help to treat her anxiety on numerous occasions, but she gave up when a therapist told her she was beyond help, as she had no recollection of a traumatic event that had started her phobia.

At the start of our therapy, Jane's heart rate was 106 beats per minute (bpm). When she was shown a picture of a Barbie doll, it soared to 141 bpm and she became tearful and distressed.

Despite Jane's insistence that she had had her phobia from birth, we established the root of her phobia in just under an hour.

Jane shared a story that she had been *told* by her dad. As a little girl, she unwrapped a doll that had been given to her as a present, and she started to cry. We explained to her that this suggested her phobia was already present.

Jane then remembered an earlier event her father had told her about. She had been playing on the floor as a toddler and started to cry. There was a doll beside her, and her dad moved it out of the way before picking Jane up. She stopped crying immediately. When her mum got home, her dad related the story and said, 'Can you believe our Jane is frightened of dolls!' Her parents kept dolls away from her from then on, telling her it was because she was scared.

We asked Jane, as a mum, what she would expect a crying child to do if their parent reached out their arms to pick them up. Jane said, 'They would probably stop crying.' We then asked her how she knew her name was Jane. She said: 'Because my parents told me that's my name.' Finally, we asked how she knew that she was scared of dolls. Jane replied: 'Because my dad told me!'

Jane suddenly realised that it was her dad who had told her she had a fear of dolls, and she'd believed him ever since.

After therapy, Jane was like a new person. We challenged her to look at the Barbie doll her daughter desperately wanted, which was covered up on the table in front of her. Jane shrugged, and with a beaming smile uncovered and picked up what had been her ultimate fear, with her heart rate remaining at 93 bpm.

Jane has since been in touch to tell us that her daughter now has a treasured doll collection, which she started with the doll Jane was able to buy on her way home from the session.

8

The Most Common Phobias

> 'Nik and Eva Speakman are two of the world's most remarkable psychotherapists. They have the most unbelievable abilities, are incredible, and more than that they are nice, nice people.'
>
> **Jeremy Kyle**

There are a number of phobias that we are asked about most frequently: in this chapter we will look at them in greater depth. However, as there are often similarities in how phobias are created, and in the process we use to help positively condition negative schemas to rid people of them, by reading the examples and tactics in this chapter you will gain a comprehensive understanding of how to overcome your own phobia.

Overwhelming Positive Evidence

The first step to conquering a fear is to learn positive facts about the thing you perceive to be causing it. This positive evidence will help you to accept that your belief has been wrong.

For example, people suffering from arachnophobia could consider the following:

* House spiders DO NOT attack humans. Spiders are cowards and fear anything bigger than them. They will always try to run away from you.

* Spiders have very poor eyesight; they only see shadows, light and dark.

* Spiders run fast as they are prey to many animals, and so they need to be able to get away quickly, to protect themselves.

* Spiders are fragile and vulnerable; their bodies are so delicate they often will not survive being dropped from a window.

* One spider can eat up to two thousand bugs and flies each year, preventing crops from being destroyed or polluted by pesticides.

* Mosquitoes carrying disease cause more human deaths than any other animal on the planet, and their number one enemy is the spider.

* Spiders don't hate you, and they definitely don't want to be near you. They only come into our homes to keep warm, perhaps find a mate and also eat any flies. Spiders seriously are the good guys.

So, think again about what is making you anxious. You can make a choice to reframe what is at the heart of your fear or unhappiness. With choice comes freedom, and our therapy will help you live free from anxiety.

Change Your Perspective

Aerophobia/Aviophobia

WHAT IS IT?

Statistics suggest that 6.5 per cent of the world's population suffer from a fear of flying, and that one passenger in every three seats on an aircraft would rather not be there. As with every phobia, aerophobia is a learned behaviour.

> 'It just seems highly unnatural to me. I've had a few messy affairs on planes. I've been lucky they haven't leaked a few [stories] of when I went bonkers. They nearly had the handcuffs out at one stage on British Airways.'
>
> **Colin Farrell**

UNDERSTANDING AND OVERCOMING AEROPHOBIA

> *Flying is the third safest mode of transport after escalators and elevators.*

There are six common reasons why someone might have a fear of flying:

1 Learned behaviour. A parent, sibling, or someone you travelled with in the past displayed fear, and you created an inaccurate schema based on their reaction. This is

especially likely if it was your first time on a plane: with no prior schema of how to behave on a plane, you would be more observant of how others behaved. If this is true for you, ask yourself: is that person always right and do you do everything they do? If not, why not?

2   Bad experience (trauma). An unpleasant experience on a flight is a common and understandable reason for developing a fear of flying. However, if you have had a bad experience, no matter how bad it was, consider what actually happened to you. Essentially, nothing bad did happen, because you are here today. If you boarded the plane to get to a destination and then got home again safely, appreciate that the plane did not let you down; it fulfilled its obligations. If your bad experience was because of turbulence, it is important to understand turbulence is normal and caused by differing temperatures that create air movement. Turbulence is no different to a bumpy road, and pilots often use those air streams to reach the destination quicker.

3   Lack of experience. Often, people fear flying due to a lack of understanding of how planes stay in the sky. But consider electricity, for example: you probably don't know exactly how that works or even what it looks like, yet you don't have any issue with flicking a switch and turning a light on. There is plenty of information online explaining the science of flight, so it may be beneficial for you to research how aeroplanes fly.

4   Terrorism. Sadly, terrorism is a concern for us all. However, past incidents have led to greatly enhanced airport security – we are now safer than ever before.

5   Other phobias. Aerophobia can be a symptom of other phobias, such as claustrophobia (a fear of enclosed spaces), emetophobia (a fear of vomit) or mysophobia (a fear of germs). Addressing the originating phobia should help to resolve your fear of flying.

6   Transference. This may occur if you have had an unrelated bad experience on an aeroplane, such as a panic attack. This creates a concern that flying could lead to another panic attack. Flying is then avoided as the panic attack has been wrongly linked to the aircraft.

Vehophobia

WHAT IS IT?

Vehophobia is the fear of driving, and it's very common. According to the National Center for Biotechnology Information in the US, up to 33 per cent of people who have experienced a car accident necessitating a hospital visit have then gone on to develop a fear of driving.[7]

LEARNING TO FEAR DRIVING

Many driving phobias are the result of having had a near miss, actually having an accident, or witnessing a near miss or accident as a passenger. Another common cause is having a panic attack in a car, leading to the car being associated with the panic attack. Often, a fear of heights can be the cause: driving over a high bridge or on a steep mountain road can trigger a rush of anxiety, creating the incorrect assumption that the car is to blame.

OVERCOMING VEHOPHOBIA

* Positive evidence. Considering the statistics will help you to upgrade and condition your inaccurate negative schema. If you passed your driving test when you were seventeen and you're now forty-five, even if you only drove somewhere once a day, you have completed 20,440 journeys. So, is it better to consider those 20,440 safe trips or focus on the one that happened to go wrong? One bad experience does not define driving.

> *While learning to walk, you stumbled many times, but it did not put you off walking.*

* Change perspective. If your fear was caused by an accident, it is important to acknowledge that you survived. Also realise that it most probably wasn't the car that caused the accident, and it might not even have been you.

* Consider an analogy. If you have ever been slicing bread and cut your finger, did you start blaming knives? No: you realised that it was just an accident.

* Consider the purpose of a car. It is a means of getting to a destination and is essentially a protective shell with an engine. Its purpose is to serve you and take you wherever you drive it.

* Panic attacks. If your fear of driving is a result of having a panic attack in the car, know that the panic attack had nothing to do with the car. A panic attack is a protection

from a perceived danger, so ask yourself: 'What was the danger when I had the panic attack?' See Chapter 6 for more information on panic disorder.

* Confidence. If you have lost confidence in your driving abilities, consider how you got your licence in the first place. You took a test where someone with exceptional experience sat with you, and after judging your ability they decided that you were fit and safe to drive. If that doesn't make you feel better, consider having some refresher lessons to give you a bit more confidence and to remind you of your ability.

* Rehearse. See yourself driving confidently in your mind's eye. This will help to build your self-esteem and confidence in driving. If you have not driven for a while, start with shorter trips, and celebrate when you get to your destination. If you feel better taking your first trips on your own, then do that. If you feel better having someone with you, then do that instead.

* Positive vibes. Music is really emotive and stimulating, so prepare some music that you find empowering, and listen to it in the car.

CASE STUDY
Sue: Vehophobia (Fear of Driving)

Sue and her husband were on their way home after a long weekend in Wales. Out of the blue, a silver car driving towards them mounted the grass kerb, came flying through the air, and ended up on top of their car.

From that moment, Sue became petrified every time she got into a car. Prior to the accident, Sue always drove, but now she could not drive at all. Even to be a passenger she had to take medication, and she could only sit in the back of the car. Sue had lost her job, and had tried counselling, CBT, eye movement desensitisation and reprocessing (EMDR), mindfulness, and pretty much whatever else she had been offered.

Before beginning our therapy, we walked Sue to our car – she became distressed and tearful, telling us she felt sick. It was clear that a combination of post-traumatic stress disorder and a phobia of driving were absolutely ruining her life.

During therapy we asked Sue how cars made her feel, and she told us they were very dangerous. When questioned about the accident, she said it had upset her greatly, and felt that it might not have happened if she and her husband had not been there.

We spoke to Sue at length about the accident to help change her perception of what had happened that day, altering her schema and removing the link she had formed to her fight-or-flight mechanism, which was causing her feelings of anxiety. Sue acknowledged that the cause of the crash was not the car; rather it was the person driving. Eventually, Sue found an entirely different perspective on cars when she realised that the thing that saved both her and her husband's life was their car. We suggested that Sue had never appreciated the fact that she and her husband had survived the crash; though their car was written off, it had protected them.

It was immediately evident from Sue's demeanour that her phobic schema had changed. When we asked her to think back to the accident now, she said she felt safe and then asked if she could get into our car. We obliged, and Sue sat in the front seat, calm and relaxed.

Feeling excited, a week after therapy Sue was able to drive again. She also told us that her sleep had improved and she was feeling better than she had in a very long time.

Emetophobia

WHAT IS IT?

Emetophobia is a fear of vomiting, and is probably the most common phobia-related inquiry we receive. According to the National Emetophobia Society, 9 per cent of the UK population, or some 5.5 million people, of whom 90–95 per cent are women, suffer from emetophobia.[8]

Our inquiries tend to fall into two categories: those who believe no one has ever heard of emetophobia and that they must be the only sufferers, and those who know all about emetophobia and believe that their case is the severest we have come across.

Emetophobia is debilitating. The consequences of this phobia usually include a fear of germs and illness. Commonly, sufferers develop an obsessive compulsive disorder around cleanliness, and take on numerous rituals in an effort to protect themselves from possible viruses and anything or anyone that has vomited or could vomit. They also often carry water, mints, antibacterial wipes and latex gloves at all times. For some people, the fear is so extreme that they become agoraphobic and are unable to leave their house.

There are currently over twenty-nine million websites dedicated to this fear and it is commonly recognised as the fifth most common fear.

youmemindbody.com

Some of the severest cases we have witnessed include a lady who gave up her child as she couldn't bear it if he was ill, a woman who rotted her teeth as she sucked on mints day and night in the belief this would prevent sickness, and another who refused to attend her daughter's university graduation and wedding.

The good news is that there is hope. We have successfully worked with hundreds of people with emetophobia, and there is no reason why anyone should have to suffer from it indefinitely.

LEARNING TO FEAR VOMIT

Most frequently, emetophobia is created in childhood. To see someone vomiting for the first time can be unpleasant, as the apparent violence of the act and the associated noises are frightening to a little one. Furthermore, if the person you see vomiting is a carer, parent or grandparent, then the perceived danger is elevated – your lack of understanding as a child often leads to a belief that your loved one is about to die, which also threatens your survival. Under these harrowing circumstances, the fight-or-flight response is activated and an inaccurate negative schema against vomit is created.

Other common instillations of emetophobia include seeing another child vomiting at school and, in the trauma of the moment, blaming and fearing sick, instead of the reason the child was sick. Alternatively, seeing a sibling being reprimanded for making a mess, or not reaching the bathroom in time to be sick, is common – no child likes getting into trouble, so vomiting becomes frightening. Being sick as a child can in itself cause emetophobia, particularly if a parent is absent or does not deal with the situation in a calm manner. An adult's reassurance that vomiting is perfectly normal is usually enough to defuse the trauma and prevent emetophobia developing.

CONDITIONING THE SCHEMA

Emetophobia is a complex phobia, but you can live a life free from it by following three steps:

1   Change your perspective. Alter your perception of the instillation event – see it for what it was and not how it felt and still feels. If you know that your emetophobia started in childhood, accept that your fear is based on a child's interpretation of what happened. Would you take a child's advice now on how to look at life and the world? If not, why not? Reanalyse the event, imagining yourself as an adult without emetophobia observing it. What actually happened? Was anybody really harmed? Updating your view of the event will help you to see it differently, and in turn to feel differently.

2   Challenge the inaccurate schema with overwhelming positive counter evidence. For example: as a baby, you often vomited and it didn't harm you. Being sick is our first line of defence against poisoning: why fear it? If you were to ingest something toxic, a doctor would administer drugs to induce vomiting and save your life. However, a phobia is an irrational fear: sufferers will start to collate evidence to justify their phobia, so they don't feel bad about having it. For example, they might search the internet for stories about people who have choked on their vomit, or news of a norovirus outbreak. This behaviour is like exercising a muscle, which over time will get bigger, and will only cultivate your emetophobia. You have to accept responsibility for conquering your fear, so make the decision to stop feeding it.

    We suggest that you focus on the opposite: from today, start looking at real evidence. Ask your friends and family when they were last sick – you will discover that it is rare, and that when it does happen it's for a good reason. This positive perspective should help to lessen your anxiety.

3 Challenge the habitual behaviours. Emetophobia can branch out to include more things to fear and avoid, such as hospitals, restaurants, schools and other public places. Make a list of all the objects and locations you consider high risk, then go through the list and challenge your justifications. For example, you might be fearful of doctors' surgeries due to the number of sick people who go there. But consider that GPs are generally healthy people who rarely take sick leave – being around sick people helps to build up a strong immune system.

It's important to step out of your comfort zone and challenge your rituals too. Write down your rituals and when you feel the need to perform them, consider your list and remind yourself that the ritual doesn't make sense, and that you don't have to do it. The list could look something like this:

* **Excessive hand washing – this makes my skin crack and leaves me more vulnerable to bacteria.**

* **Using a hot water bottle – this doesn't prevent sickness; it warms and relaxes my muscles, but it doesn't have any anti-nausea qualities.**

* **Washing clothes every time I go outside – a sterile environment will deplete my immune system and make me more susceptible to catching viruses.**

You have got a journey ahead of you. Every journey starts with one small step. If you can do more, great – but if you can't, doing just one small thing you couldn't do yesterday will make you realise you are OK, you are safe, and you can build on it tomorrow.

CASE STUDY
Charlie: Emetophobia (Fear of Vomit)

Charlie had suffered from emetophobia for as long as she could remember, but it was progressively getting worse. Charlie worked with children and revealed how challenging it was when they got sick – she would spend the following two weeks overanalysing everything, terrified that she would become sick. She would cancel her plans, eat bland food and refuse alcohol, dashing away from social events early. If she was in a busy area, she would be constantly scanning to see if anyone looked like they were about to be sick, so that she could get out of the way as quickly as possible.

Emetophobia for Charlie was like carrying a burden around with her all the time.

Charlie came to one of our workshops, hoping we could help. When speaking to someone, we are constantly looking for clues to identify the root of any anxiety disorder, and after asking Charlie a few questions, we identified that it wasn't just the sickness phobia that was hindering her; it was the idea of needing to get home, to a place of safety.

We asked Charlie whether she had ever been away from home and hadn't been able to get back, or was actually unwell and couldn't return home. She remembered an incident when she was ten: she had gone away for a few days' holiday with a friend's family, but was so homesick and anxious that it made her physically vomit. Charlie revealed that she was so distressed her parents came and picked her up, which was upsetting for everyone involved, and embarrassing for her.

After the workshop, Charlie completed a timeline (see page 19) to identify the life events that had created her anxiety-causing schemas. As a result, she realised that before the holiday she had been feeling very anxious as her dad had recently been diagnosed with cancer. Suddenly everything fell into place. Being aware of illness and death for the first time, she became afraid that her family were in danger and going to die. From then on, she never liked to be away from home.

Furthermore, Charlie's timeline helped her identify another contributing factor. Within twenty-four hours of moving out of home to start university aged nineteen, her best friend was killed in a car accident, and Charlie had to rush back to deal with death and heartache again. Had she blamed being away from home for her trauma?

Having identified the two significant events her issues stemmed from, Charlie began to process them. She had not dealt with either, instead burying her emotional pain. She made an effort to talk things through with her partner, friends and family – initially this was very hard for her, but the more she did it, the lighter her burden felt. Discussing the original events with other adults gave her alternative perspectives to consider, enabling her to look back and see things differently. She saw how one event had built up and then magnified the other, and how her resulting behaviours fed her phobia.

Once she had changed her perspective and challenged her habits, her phobia disappeared.

Charlie came to share her success at another workshop, saying she knew it had gone when she volunteered to clean up a child's vomit at work, with no fear or repercussions. She explained that she was now able to eat more food, make more plans and not worry about them. She recalled feeling sick a few months ago and described it as the most liberating experience – she thought, 'If I'm going to be sick, that's fine. My body is doing what it needs to do, and I will feel better afterwards.' Then her nausea vanished because she wasn't stressed about it.

Now her phobia had gone, she realised it was the anxiety caused by the phobia that made her feel nauseous. Life without emetophobia was a much happier and far safer place to be for Charlie.

Since attending your Manchester workshop for my severe phobia of vomit, life has been so different. I got back from a family holiday and didn't think every day about vomit – it was amazing! I don't have to plan out my day and routes so I can avoid situations that would trigger my anxiety. If anyone is on the fence about attending, please don't be; I went on my own and it's the best thing I have ever done.

Amanda

9

Social Anxiety

I don't think any words can ever express just how much you have helped me, and changed my life and thoughts for the better. Now, thanks to you, I have a future and I am going to grab it with both hands. You showed me how I have misunderstood situations from my past which were keeping me locked away. You simply guided my thought process to a better and healthier way of thinking, to release me from my past and my negative thoughts and behaviours. You both really are amazing and an inspiration.

Ashlea

Social anxiety is the fear of social situations that involve interaction with other people. You could say social anxiety is the fear and anxiety of being negatively judged and evaluated by other people.

socialphobia.org

Glossophobia is the medical term for the fear of public speaking and is a social phobia, or social anxiety disorder.

healthline.com

Recent studies suggest that Body Dysmorphic Disorder (BDD) may share some key similarities with Social Anxiety Disorder (SAD), including diagnostic features, prevalence, and treatment overlap. A new study of Body Dysmorphic Disorder among adults with SAD revealed that treatment for SAD can also reduce symptoms of BDD.

anxiety.org

Social anxiety is our primary focus in this chapter, but we will also cover glossophobia and body dysmorphic disorder.

What is Social Anxiety?

Social anxiety, previously known as 'social phobia', affects millions of people all over the world. It can impede everyday tasks such as presentations at work or university, a team talk to a group of colleagues, or simple activities that the majority of the population take for granted, like socialising with friends or interacting with a shop assistant.

According to the US Social Anxiety Institute, social anxiety disorder is the third largest psychological disorder in the country, and it is estimated that the likelihood of developing it is as high as 13–14 per cent. The National Institute for Health and Care Excellence estimates this figure at 12 per cent in UK.[9] Social anxiety disorder tends to have a higher prevalence in women.

For people with social anxiety, their fear is often of being the centre of attention, or of others noticing their anxious behaviour. This can create a fear of behaving in an embarrassing or humiliating way, which leads to withdrawal from social situations. Some of the worst cases we have encountered have been a lady who ran out of a hair salon with her hair dripping wet as the social interaction was just too much, and another who couldn't walk through the door of her doctor's surgery despite her alarming health condition.

In this chapter we will discuss the various elements of social anxiety and share how you can address your own anxiety and discomfort.

Glossophobia

Glossophobia, a fear of public speaking, is considered to be the number one fear in the world, and a recent YouGov survey suggested that 20 per cent of Britons are too afraid to speak publicly.[10] The survey also revealed that women are twice as likely as men to be 'very afraid' of public speaking.

Glossophobia can also be described as stage fright or performance anxiety, and holds people back in many different ways. It can ruin events that should be a positive and exciting experience, such as a birthday party, a best man speech, or walking down the aisle as a bride.

Surprisingly, research shows that people with severe social anxiety say they would rather die than speak in front of a group of people.[11]

> **'If you go to a funeral, you're better off in the casket than doing the eulogy.'**
>
> **Jerry Seinfeld**

> **'There are times I remember before I walked on stage, where if I had the choice of walking on stage or dying, I would have chosen death. The underlying reason for the fear was the extreme pressure to be perfect.'**
>
> **Donny Osmond**

Body Dysmorphic Disorder

Body dysmorphic disorder (BDD) affects approximately 1.7–2.4 per cent of the US population and around 0.5–0.7 per cent of the UK population.[12]

The condition, which causes obsessive thinking about a flaw that is either imagined or hardly noticeable, usually surfaces in the teenage years, with social media appearing to contribute. Many people with BDD find themselves compulsively checking their perceived flaw, and so this condition has also been linked to obsessive compulsive disorder.

Whereas most individuals might be merely annoyed by a real or imagined physical imperfection, sufferers from BDD are likely to spend hours a day worrying about it, or taking excessive measures such as surgery to address it.

Sufferers may also feel a need to hide the flaw or even themselves from others, leading to social isolation, depression and sometimes agoraphobia.

The Origin of Social Anxieties

In an interview with Diane Sawyer, Barbra Streisand opened up about her decades-long battle with performance anxiety. Her social phobia began in 1967 when she forgot the lyrics to one of her songs during a live performance in New York's Central Park.

> 'I didn't sing and charge people for twenty-seven years because of that night . . . I was like, "God, I don't know. What if I forget the words again?"'
>
> **Barbra Streisand**

The good news is that social anxieties are not a genetic or biological condition; none have to be a lifelong affliction as all are a learned behaviour, often formed in childhood and particularly in the teenage years.

Whether you are socially anxious, cannot speak publicly or have BDD, the likely culprits are:

* **Being bullied by someone at school, home or work, and as a result wanting to disappear from view or keep a low profile.**

* **Being laughed at and humiliated because of something you said or mispronounced, for example, when reading out loud in class.**

* **Being made to feel worthless and inadequate by an abusive parent, friend or partner.**

* **Comparing yourself to others and chastising yourself for not being as good, clever, articulate or beautiful as them.**

* **Comparing your life negatively to other people's lives on social media, overlooking the fact that these images are usually enhanced or exaggerated, and that people rarely post details of the bad things in their lives.**

* **Comparing your possessions to others' and feeling like a failure if they materially appear to have more than you.**

* **Experiencing immense embarrassment. If you fall over as a child, you dust yourself off and get straight back up again, but as a teenager or adult, the first thing you do is look around and think, 'Oh no, did anyone see me?'**

Overcoming Social Anxieties

To overcome your social anxieties, you need to:

1 Locate the origin of your belief.

2 Challenge the origin of your belief: what you believed may not be true now, or was never true.

3 Practise and rehearse being confident.

4 Build genuine self-confidence.

If you suffer from social anxiety, who made you feel this way? Who belittled you, laughed at you or made you feel inferior? This is the root of your issue: it's why you feel you need to keep away from people to protect yourself from these negative emotions. However, it is unfair to penalise others and deprive them of your company because of the action of one or a few. Expecting everyone to be no different to the perpetrator(s) of your social anxiety is both unfair and inaccurate.

Also, please consider that bullying is not a personal issue: it was not directed just at you. Bullies bully. They live their life treating everyone in the same way – either it's what they have been taught at home, or it's due to their own rock bottom self-esteem. They try to elevate their own status by attacking or reducing other people's. Alternatively, it's because they fear losing you as they feel you are too good for them – if they make you feel worthless, then you are more likely to feel grateful to them, and are therefore more likely to stick around.

If you are suffering from glossophobia, why did you choose to blame public speaking? If your fear stems from a teacher who humiliated you in class, then it wasn't speaking out that caused your discomfort, it was the teacher. To alter your perception and condition your schema, you need to re-examine the original event, seeing it for what it was, and not how it felt in that moment. If the teacher reprimanded you and you were embarrassed, then perhaps the teacher was just having a bad day, or in a class of thirty mistakenly thought you were responsible for something.

If you have BDD, did someone at school make you feel bad about yourself? Or perhaps you were envious of someone. Whatever the reason, understanding the origin of your issue will help you to challenge and positively condition it. For example, if you had a crush on a boy at school who then spurned you, you will undoubtedly have questioned why. If you have a physical feature that you dislike, you might have blamed this to justify the rejection. Look for a positive element of the rejection: for example, would you still be interested in that boy today? Childhood crushes rarely last – the rejection might have saved you from wasting your time.

Here are some exercises to help make a positive difference:

REHEARSE

To help overcome your fear, consider rehearsing before you socialise or speak. Close your eyes and visualise yourself delivering a perfect speech and receiving a warm reception from your audience, or interacting with an engaged group of friends. Doing this a number of times gives your brain the message that you have already done it, and that it went really well. Your brain cannot tell the difference between something you have actually done and something you have strongly visualised or rehearsed.

SIGH

A simple but effective coping technique is to give an emotive sigh before you speak or socialise. This signals to your brain and body that the task has been completed. An emotive sigh, is a sigh out loud that engages your whole body and your emotions. Picture the event and score your fear out of ten. Then, while holding that picture in your mind's eye, sigh. Then sigh again, allowing your shoulders to drop and relax, and then again, sinking into your seat. Keep sighing until thinking about the event gives you no fear or your fear is reduced.

PREPARE

Write down some topics you can talk confidently about and use them to start conversations when you're socialising, such as popular TV shows or hobbies you're passionate about. This can act like a security blanket. Once you build a rapport with someone, it's amazing how quickly your insecurities and anxieties can disappear. One of the most common rapport builders in the UK is talking about the weather!

USE PROPS

Give yourself as many comfort props as possible. If you're delivering a speech, using index cards to read from is perfectly acceptable and an effective prompt. It also helps if there is somebody in the audience or in your social circle who you love and trust, so that you can direct your eyes to them for reassurance and comfort. And finally, remember that if you're talking about something people want to hear, they will listen.

Self-Esteem

A significant component of social anxiety issues is low self-esteem. But how you perceive yourself is largely based on how other people have made you feel about yourself. Your social anxiety, glossophobia or BDD could be the result of your self-esteem having been knocked by someone else.

It is common to overlook your own qualities and attributes, seeing yourself through a lens of negativity imposed by others, without ever questioning their motive. What were their intentions? Examples to consider are:

* **They were jealous of you.**

* **They were worried that you would steal their limelight.**

* **They were worried that if you became too confident you might leave them and they would lose you.**

* **They were worried that you would supersede them in life.**

* **They had low self-esteem and felt bad about themselves, so being unkind gave them a feeling of power.**

> *When you change the way you look at circumstances, the circumstances you look at begin to change.*

Also consider that you yourself might have misread a situation. For example, you may have overheard a conversation and thought that someone was speaking negatively about you when they were actually talking about someone else, and this misunderstanding could have affected your self-esteem.

Here are some tips to build your self-esteem, which in turn will help to increase your confidence:

* Write down a list of the people who have made you feel bad. Were they a school bully, parent, teacher, colleague, partner, ex?

* Now look at the list and consider whether they are still a part of your life. If not, either they have moved on or you have moved on. Either way, they are in the past. Just as you have moved on with your life, you need to move on with your emotions too.

> *The past is history and while history cannot be changed, your perception of it can be, any time you choose.*

* If they are still in your life, consider whether you can distance yourself from them. If not, tell them how they make you feel – you could write them a letter or speak to them in private. If you can't change them, you must change how you deal with them. For example, if they are very negative to you, try being excessively positive in return. If they criticise you, say, 'That was hurtful, but I'll assume you're having a bad day as I know you're too nice to be intentionally mean.' A different approach will provide a different result.

* Look at the list again, and ask yourself what skills, qualities or qualifications each person has or had to judge you. Why would you choose to allow their views to tarnish your view of yourself?

* Next consider whether each person on the list was being kind to you. Unless the situation was a total misunderstanding, they can't possibly have been, if they made you feel bad. Ask yourself why you would want to carry unkind opinions around with you. If you are speaking to yourself negatively using their words, or as a consequence of their actions, you are reinforcing the original unkindness. If you see yourself as a kind person, remember this includes being kind to yourself.

* Think about the motives of the people who judged you, referring to the examples on page 139. It is important to accept that you may have been their victim then, but today you are a victor.

* Realise that if you have ever been loved this is because you are lovable. Whether they are a parent, sibling, friend or even a pet, consider the reasons why they love or loved you. Focus on the moments when they have expressed their love, and imagine yourself floating into their body and seeing yourself through their eyes – as the truly incredible person that you really are.

CASE STUDY
Karen: Social Anxiety (Fear of People)

Karen had severe social anxiety, which she described as a phobia of 'dealing with people'.

Karen worked with her husband David as a school cleaner: the only job where no one else would be around. However, if she ever walked into a classroom and saw a teacher who had stayed late, she would break down. Karen was struggling to hold on to her job, and she relied on David for everything. They rarely left the house; even being around her own family made Karen uncomfortable. She felt a huge amount of guilt for not seeing her children and grandchildren, despite them living minutes away – the last photograph she had with any of them was taken ten years ago.

For years Karen had tried medication, counselling and self-help books, but nothing had worked. She was desperate to get over her social anxiety, but she felt powerless to control her fears.

When Karen came to our clinic for therapy, we asked her why people scared her. She said she feared she would say or do something stupid, and that they would judge her. We wanted to understand why Karen believed David was the only person in the world not judging her. She said she thought it was because she knew that he loved her and understood her problems, whereas other people didn't and would judge her because of them.

Prior to our therapy, we had asked Karen's family to send us letters for her. We read them to Karen during the session. One of her grandchildren wrote: 'I love you, Nan, but we don't get to see you much. I want to have dinner with you and go and feed the ducks.' Karen was upset because she hadn't realised her grandchildren wanted to see her.

Karen's son wrote: 'Mum, I think you are very special. Since the children were born, we haven't seen you as much as we would like to, and the kids need you in our lives. We all miss the way you were; a happy, loving mother.'

Karen's daughter wrote: 'Mum, you will probably find our letters hard to read but we need you to know how much love and support we have for you. It is really hard knowing that you have missed out on so much in all our lives. We want nothing more than you to enjoy having time with the grandchildren. I personally would love to have a girly day out for lunch and go shopping, but I know at the moment that is too much. Please know we are all here for you, but most of all we just want our mum back.'

Karen was surprised because she hadn't felt she was important to her family, but she said it was lovely to hear. She agreed there was no judgement from them. For years she had believed something that was untrue, and now she was hearing the facts.

We made a list with Karen of all the people who mattered in her life. We asked how many of them were judging her, taking into consideration that she hadn't found time for any of them over the last decade. She looked through the list and she revealed that none of them were judging her, despite having missed so many milestones in their lives. We told Karen that she faced a choice; to believe something that wasn't true and walk away from her family, or to look at the facts and take her family back today. They loved her so much that they were prepared to keep their distance, to make her life more bearable. Karen had never considered this before, and her perspective of how loved she was began to change.

Then we asked Karen who had taken away her self-esteem. At first she said herself, but when we explained that low self-esteem often stems from childhood, Karen revealed that she was bullied at school – the whole class had turned against her and stopped talking to her for two weeks.

We needed Karen to look at the situation again, but consider an alternative positive perspective. Karen realised that she hadn't been entirely ignored, and it hadn't actually been everyone in the class. When the bullying stopped, Karen had continued to be unkind to herself, using it as a model for how she must be treated.

Karen was finally able to accept that she was a very loved lady. Later that day, Karen was able to meet her whole family in a restaurant, which would have been unthinkable before. For the first time in years, they were all together.

Karen now sees her family every week. She loves spending time with her grandchildren and no longer works with David – she is a manager in a department store, dealing face to face with staff and the public daily.

CASE STUDY
Maria: Glossophobia (Fear of Public Speaking)

Meeting bubbly, confident company director Maria, it was hard to believe that she had a problem with public speaking.

We met Maria in the boardroom at her office, where she explained that she had no issue talking to one person, or even two, three or four people – but any more than that and she would panic and faint. As a result, Maria had to employ someone to speak on her behalf at talks, events and business meetings. She felt that her fear was holding her back and that she was letting down herself and her team. Maria had the knowledge and skill to expand her business, but she would need to present and pitch in order to secure bigger clients.

We asked Maria to tell us how she felt if she had to make a speech. She said she was worried she would 'mess it up and embarrass herself'. She had used the same words earlier, and for us, those words were a key piece of evidence to determine how her fear started. We asked when in her life she had 'messed up and embarrassed herself'. She immediately responded: 'When I fainted as I was about to deliver a presentation for a business contract.'

We explained that, for her to have had this phobic response at that moment, the phobia must already have been present. We asked Maria to think back to when she was a little girl. Had she ever spoken in front of a group, become embarrassed or made a mistake? It was evident from Maria's eye movement that she was searching through a magnitude of her schemas, when suddenly it came flooding back.

The Brownies are the section of the long-running UK Girlguiding organisation for girls aged seven to ten. To officially become a Brownie, Maria would have to stand up in front of her group to recite the Brownie Promise.

Maria's mum had been given a sheet of paper with Maria's lines, which Maria had learned by heart. With the girls all sitting in a circle, this was Maria's big moment. Excitedly, she stood up and recited the words impeccably. She still remembered them word for word now. Beaming with pride, Maria was delighted with her efforts. The group leader (known as Brown Owl) nodded approvingly and said, 'Well done Maria, that was wonderful. Now can you read the second part?'

What second part? Maria had not been told about a second part!

Needless to say, this moment of joy instantly became a moment of trauma. Maria was now standing in front of the group, getting more and more embarrassed as she had no words for Brown Owl. In that moment, Maria's glossophobia was created.

Maria hadn't thought about that event for some time, but she was very distressed to recall the embarrassment and shame she had felt. It was obvious that she was still seeing the event through the eyes of her seven-year-old self, feeling the same horror.

To help Maria, we had to change her perspective of that event, helping her to see it for what it actually was and not how it felt, so as to condition the negative schema. Maria confirmed that her mum had not been given the second part, and she had only learned what she'd been given. We asked Maria if she had therefore complied with everything she had been asked to do. Maria said yes. We then asked if she had been excited to recite the Promise. She said she had put so much work into learning it, because she wanted Brown Owl to see how committed she was to the Brownies. We asked Maria if she had not only complied, but also excelled at delivering her lines. She said yes. We asked if she could have learned the second part and recited it just as well as the first, if it had been given to her. She said yes, of course. So, we asked, who was actually at fault for the entire situation? 'Brown Owl,' Maria said. Had public speaking created her embarrassment? If not, who had? Again, Maria said it was Brown Owl. So who actually messed up that day? She said, 'Brown Owl.' Knowing that Brown Owl messed up by forgetting to give Maria's mum the second part of her recital, who should have felt embarrassed? 'Brown Owl.'

With this epiphany, Maria said, 'I had never thought of it like that before. I did what I was supposed to, and I did a great job.'

The following day, we sat in a lecture theatre at the University of East Anglia, watching Maria deliver a humorous, engaging and informative twenty-minute talk to 350 business students. Maria had every person in the theatre mesmerised. She was so confident that the professor of business studies asked if she would come back and speak to another group. We were overjoyed!

CASE STUDY
Karlette: Body Dysmorphic Disorder

Karlette had been brutally attacked when she was just fifteen. What started as a playground argument escalated to an out-of-school conflict. While out shopping one Saturday, a car pulled up and two women jumped out. They started to hit Karlette – first her face, then her ribs. They ripped a chunk of hair from Karlette's scalp while smashing her into a wall, causing a broken cheekbone, fractured ribs and severe bruising to her head.

Now twenty-two, Karlette had moved away from her hometown and started to self-harm. Her mother shared how her daughter's personality had changed drastically after the attack. Karlette's image had become an obsession. She wouldn't leave the house without a full face of make-up to hide behind, and would spend literally hours making herself up.

Karlette told us that she had been studying at a stage school and had wanted to be a TV presenter, but her confidence was shattered. Her sister joined us, adding that Karlette had gone from a bubbly, outgoing young teenager to a recluse.

It was evident that Karlette had post-traumatic stress disorder and the attack had caused body dysmorphic disorder. She believed on some level that she was to blame and deserved to be attacked, which had left her ugly and disfigured. The truth was that her scars from the attack had faded; her self-inflicted wounds were now far more visible.

We began therapy by asking Karlette what she saw when she looked in the mirror without make-up. She said she only saw someone with scars. When we asked what the scars meant to her, she said they make her feel weak. We asked her to describe her faults; she said, 'The scars.' She went on to say that she thought one of her eyes had drooped since the attack. We gently explained that she was the only one who could see that – because it was not there. She agreed and said, 'You're right, I feel a little silly about that now.' This showed us that her self-image schema was starting to change and become positively conditioned.

We asked Karlette if she had been inviting the women who attacked her back into her life over the last seven years to continue their assault. She said no. When asked who had been attacking her since then, Karlette thought for a moment and then responded, 'Me.' We told Karlette that what those girls had done to her was incredibly wrong and that it should never have happened, but we pointed out that the attack had lasted only minutes that one day – while Karlette had carried on attacking herself for seven years.

Karlette was having a deep moment of realisation; we could see her start to sit up straighter, with more confidence. We asked who had done the most damage to her, and she replied, 'Me.' We asked if she deserved to get hurt by two people who were considerably older than her, and she said no. We asked if what they did was wrong, and she said yes. We asked if what she was doing now was wrong, and she firmly said yes again.

We suggested that the attackers had moved on with their lives, yet she hadn't moved on with hers. We showed Karlette a picture of herself taken just after the attack, and pointed out that the image she had been seeing in the mirror for the last seven years was still the same one. She agreed that she had trapped herself in that moment, with that image. It was time to let this image go, and allow the girl in the photo to heal.

Karlette had carried on from where the girls left off: they hurt her once, and she had hurt herself every day since. We wanted Karlette to see what we and everyone else saw – not a beaten-up girl but a beautiful woman. We removed the photo, revealing a mirror behind it. Karlette looked at herself and smiled. Now when we asked her to think back to the attack, she revealed she felt fine, and confused by feeling fine. She began to laugh; at this point we knew she had overcome her PTSD and BDD.

Some time after therapy, Karlette contacted us to say her confidence had improved so much that she had volunteered for a charity programme, building orphanages in Africa. No make-up required! In 2016, Karlette won the title of Miss Greater London. She then met her future husband, and she is now married with a young son. She uses her story to help other people with mental health issues.

10

Health Anxiety

You cured my phobia of death. I recently found out my Nanna Lill has cancer, so the fact I could visit her at her nursing home meant even more to me than before. I cannot put into words just what you have done for me. Everybody I know noticed a difference in me immediately after seeing you both, and I have never felt better. What you both do to help people like me is amazing. I wish I could express my gratitude more.

Gemma

We all worry about our health from time to time. This is understandable – for example, if you need surgery, or if you are recalled by your doctor following medical tests. Equally, being worried about a loved one with a real health concern is normal. Indeed, there can be benefits to being mindful of our health, which often prompts us to make positive lifestyle changes, such as drinking less alcohol and taking up exercise. But when health dominates our thoughts and we catastrophise every niggle, this is health anxiety, which should be addressed.

Health anxiety is common. A recent study found that the NHS could save more than £420m a year if it were to offer treatment for health anxiety and cyberchondria (a psychological ailment caused by people obsessively looking up their symptoms on the internet). The researchers estimated that at least one in five people attending hospital outpatient appointments suffered from health anxiety.[13]

What is Health Anxiety?

Health anxiety was previously referred to as hypochondria, and is an obsessive, exaggerated and irrational worry about having a serious medical condition.

This anxiety disorder is entirely about the psychological reaction to ill health, whether it exists or not.

> **Those affected by health anxiety have an obsessional preoccupation with the idea that they are currently (or will be) experiencing a physical illness. The most common health anxieties tend to centre on conditions such as cancer, HIV, AIDS, etc. However, the person experiencing health anxiety may fixate on any type of illness.**
>
> **Anxiety UK**

Often a person with health anxiety will exaggerate niggles, aches, pains, pins and needles, or unusual bodily sensations, and will fixate on their symptoms, imagining the worst-case scenario. Many will also spend a significant amount of time researching ailments and diseases, looking for the most severe and sinister possibility to explain a minor or even normal body sensation. They will often self-diagnose and go on to imagine, create or convince themselves of the symptoms they have read about.

> *You become what you think about most.*

Reassurance from doctors or others is usually futile.

Causes of Health Anxiety

Health anxiety is learned or self-created, and manifests most often as a result of:

* A parent or family member with health anxiety teaching you to always look for the worst-case scenario and obsess about health.

* An overprotective parent who may have rewarded you with affection and attention when you were ill.

* A parent or family member who may have worried a lot about your health when you were young.

* An illness or death in the family.

* A personal experience of a serious health concern or illness.

Symptoms of Health Anxiety

There are various symptoms, behaviours and thoughts a person with health anxiety may display, including the following:

* Constantly worrying about health

* Constantly concentrating on feelings in the body

* Frequently searching for ailments and symptoms

* Feelings of anxiety with every pain, niggle or unusual feeling

* Not accepting when a doctor tells you that you are well

* Dwelling on whether your doctor may have missed something

* Worrying that your test results may have been mixed up

* Frequently feeling unwell

* Belief that something is terribly wrong with you all the time

* Frequently requiring visits to the doctor

* Struggling to watch hospital- or health-related TV shows

* Searching for symptoms in yourself when reading or hearing about an illness

* Feelings of panic if you hear someone has cancer, or a terminal illness

* Always jumping to the worst-case scenario, e.g. 'this could be cancer'

* Carrying many medications with you 'just in case'

* Needing to know the closest hospital and doctors surgery at all times

* Talking about ailments often, with the intention of gaining reassurance from others

Overcoming Health Anxiety

Before you can cure yourself of this particular issue, it is important to acknowledge that your anxiety is learned. When your anxious feelings begin to manifest, remind yourself that you feel as you do because of the person or event that created your anxiety. Also be mindful of spending too much time with friends whose primary topic of conversation is health.

Challenge the origin

Consider where your negative health schema came from. Ask yourself: how may I have learned my fear? Am I repeating a behaviour I have witnessed? Did someone I know have health anxiety or always jump to the worst possible conclusion? Was I ever seriously ill? Was someone close to me seriously ill? Did someone close to me die?

Once you identify the event or person that helped create your health anxiety, challenge it with alternative positive evidence. Ask yourself why you are choosing to repeat that person's behaviour. Are they always right? Do they have medical qualifications? If not, why should you follow their lead on this? What are their motives for being so health conscious and do they apply to me? Do I want to continue the cycle of health anxiety when it's so detrimental?

This is an important moment that takes us back to the core message of our therapy: you have a choice. As you'll see from the following suggestions, even faced with upsetting and life-changing situations, you can choose to focus on the positive:

I WAS SERIOUSLY ILL

Remember: you got better. You, more than most, have the evidence and personal proof that even if you are seriously ill you can still recover.

SOMEONE CLOSE TO ME WAS SERIOUSLY ILL

Why would someone else's health issue be a risk to you? Are you the same age? Have you had the same diet for your entire life? Have you had the same lifestyle and experiences as them?

SOMEONE CLOSE TO ME DIED OR NEARLY DIED

If they did not die, they got better – proving that serious health issues can be overcome.

If they did die, consider how you differ from them. Are you genetically identical? Do you live in an identical environment, doing, eating and surrounding yourself with exactly the same things as them? The answer, of course, is no: we are all individuals. Focus on the differences and they will help relieve your anxiety.

Change your perspective

If you suffer from health anxiety, you see only death, near death or terminal illness as the outcome of illness. However, this is far from the case; it is important to seek out positive counter evidence. For example, instead of googling your ailments, try googling someone who survived the particular illness you're concerned about.

A helpful analogy is to view your body as a car; the vehicle that enables you to travel through your life. If your car were to break down or develop a fault, you wouldn't assume it was ready to be scrapped. Apply this reasoning to your body. If your car were to start making an odd tapping noise, this would be a warning that something needed to be fixed. On occasion, your body may provide you with a message that you should take it a little easier, eat better, rest more, or go and see a doctor. Ill health is your body's way of communicating with you: be grateful that you have such an amazing protective system. Surely it would be far worse if we never received any warning that something in our body was wrong.

CASE STUDY
Christine: Health Anxiety

Christine attended one of our workshops hoping to find some information to help her health anxiety, but she was not expecting a cure. Even a small improvement would give her some respite from her anxiety, which dominated her thoughts from morning till night.

In one of the breaks, Christine came over to speak with us, explaining her symptoms. We asked what she thought may have been the cause. Christine told us that she had been very ill, and had faced death unless a liver donor was found. Fortunately, she was gifted with life when a compatible liver became available and she had a successful transplant. However, although her life had been saved, from that day Christine had been preoccupied by her health. She had faced death once; now she was waiting for the next illness to come along and end her life. Every little ache or odd feeling became Christine's focus. Anxiety would sweep over her like a wave, and she would fight to come up, gasping for breath. She had been given life but she wasn't living.

We said to her: 'There are always two ways to look at life. You can either choose to think, "I'm going to die one day," or you can choose to think, "Because I know I'm going to die one day, I'm going to live my life as much as possible, to the best of my ability."' We went on to point out that Christine had been given a second chance. We said: 'The fact you still think you are ill means you are not just wasting your life – you are also disrespecting the person that gave you a second chance at life, and you are too kind to do that.'

Christine thought for a moment and realised that, while she had been given the chance of a tomorrow, her donor had not. She was throwing away the gift of life. To honour her donor, she made the decision not to take her life for granted anymore, or to dwell on illness, as she had personal proof that you can get better.

We had helped Christine to update and condition her negative health schema, and coupled with the goal-setting session to give new direction and purpose, Christine walked out of our workshop free from health anxiety.

CASE STUDY
Lizzy: Health Anxiety

Lizzy was shaking when she approached us during one of our workshops. She sobbed as she told us that her grandfather had died when she was twelve, and a part of her had died that day too.

Lizzy adored her grandfather. He made her laugh, listened to her natter endlessly about anything and everything, read to her, watched movies with her, and played board games with her. However, no one had told her that he was ill. One day he was there; the next he had died. At that moment, Lizzy created a schema that death could happen unexpectedly at any moment, and from then on, Lizzy was convinced she was going to die.

Now a wife and mum, she was frantic as she had realised her own daughter was starting to copy her health behaviours, and her marriage was suffering too. They hadn't taken a holiday abroad since their honeymoon, as Lizzy needed to be near a hospital at all times and was concerned about language barriers if she were to fall ill.

Lizzy looked completely broken as she said, 'I know you say it is learned, but it's dominated over twenty years of my life, so I don't know how you could ever help me to think any differently.' Lizzy's story was all too common: we felt it should be relatively easy to change her perspective.

We asked how Lizzy's grandfather had died, and Lizzy told us that he had died of lung cancer. We asked if he had known he had lung cancer. She said yes. We asked if he had known for a while. She said she later learned that he had. Then we asked: 'So his death was unexpected and sudden?'

Lizzy froze for a moment. Then she said, 'No, no he didn't die suddenly. He had been unwell for some time, but the family decided not to tell me. I've never considered that before.'

We also asked how old Lizzy was now – thirty-three; how old her granddad was when he died – seventy-six; whether he smoked – he did; whether she smoked – she didn't; and why she thought he had lung cancer – because he smoked. Finally we asked Lizzy to think again about what had actually killed her grandfather. She replied: 'Cigarettes.'

Then she started to smile as she said, 'Death wasn't to blame, the cigarettes were – and I don't smoke.'

We finished our chat by asking Lizzy how her granddad would feel, knowing that not admitting to her that he was dying had ruined her life. Lizzy said he would be devastated. We asked if she was ready to honour him and enjoy the life he would have wanted her to have. Lizzy firmly replied, 'Yes.'

Our questioning had helped Lizzy to look at the evidence and condition her own health anxiety schema. Some weeks later, Lizzy emailed to say that she had booked a family holiday and was too busy working on her goals to waste any more time dwelling on ill health.

CASE STUDY
Louise: Health Anxiety

Louise moved from Newcastle to Australia to work as a personal trainer. When one of her clients, who had become a friend, was diagnosed with a rare form of cancer and needed a kidney transplant, Louise selflessly donated a kidney to save his life.

But ten months later, Louise was readmitted to hospital with a bowel obstruction. She was told she had been an hour away from death. During this traumatic time, her younger brother died unexpectedly in his sleep, leaving Louise with an all-encompassing fear of dying, and concerned that she would be unable to survive with only one kidney.

Her fear and anxiety became so severe that she had no option but to return home to live with her family. Soon she started to suffer panic attacks and, frightened to be alone, she became reliant on her father, who became her full-time carer, even sleeping by her side.

During therapy, we presented Louise with positive evidence to condition her schema, encouraging her to appreciate that she was healthier and stronger than she thought. We pointed out how healthy her kidney must have been to enable her to be a donor. Indeed, her doctor in Australia had told her it was the best kidney he had ever seen, even saying she was born to donate a kidney. When we asked what that told her about the kidney she had left, she acknowledged that 'it must be a really good one'.

To reinforce this message, we took Louise to a local medical centre, where the GP shared data to suggest that donors live longer than non-donors. He also told Louise that she was in the top 3 per cent of the population in terms of fitness, and explained that many people do not even realise that they have only one fully functioning kidney. Therefore, to some degree, her donated kidney was surplus to requirements. His only advice was to request a check-up every six months: a formality as opposed to a necessity.

Throughout the course of our therapy, we identified Louise's issues so each could be addressed individually. The original issue was post-traumatic stress disorder, which had then led to:

* **Monophobia – a fear of being alone in case she were to die**

* **Thanatophobia – a fear of death**

* **Sitophobia – a fear of food that could harm her and cause death**

* **Obsessive compulsive disorder**

* **Health anxiety**

Louise had never feared for her life until she returned to the hospital in unbearable pain and was told, 'If you do not have an operation within the next hour, you could die.' At this moment she was on her own. Her brother had been alone too when he died in his sleep. This triggered the need to have someone by her side constantly, just in case the worst happened.

However, when Louise began to look at what had happened to her rationally, she was able to come to terms with it. She accepted that she had been told she could die, but she was actually OK. She also understood that the bowel obstruction was caused by the operation to donate her kidney – since it was impossible for her to donate another kidney as she only had one left, this risk had been totally eliminated.

A few months later, Louise sent us an update on how her life had changed since seeing us. She had started a couple of her own businesses and reignited her passion for personal training, taking on new clients in England and online from Australia. Louise now lives independently, with her dad no longer needing to be her carer.

Remembering our key steps to refocusing on the positives, write down your answers to these questions, to help you make the right choices and take control of your situation:

* **What was the origin of my health anxiety?**

* **How did I learn to become anxious about my health?**

* **Does that reason still apply?**

* **In what ways am I different from the person who caused my health anxiety?**

* **In what ways is my negative schema inaccurate?**

* **What would be more beneficial for me to consider and believe?**

11

Obsessive Compulsive Disorder

Thank you so much for an amazing day. You are so inspirational and I can honestly say I came home and just stopped my OCD rituals. Just like that: 'I have no magical powers!'

Vanessa

Anxiety can manifest itself in many different ways. One such manifestation is obsessive compulsive disorder. We are seeing ever more cases of this debilitating condition, and it's so moving to see what a difference our therapy is making to people who are consumed by it. In this chapter, we will guide you to freedom from the grasp of OCD.

What is OCD?

Obsessive compulsive disorder (OCD) is an anxiety-related condition that manifests as an overwhelming need to perform a certain behaviour, which the sufferer feels has to be done to avoid grave consequences.

According to OCD UK, this disorder affects 1.2 per cent of the UK population (three quarters of a million people), and the Anxiety and Depression Association of America states that OCD affects 1 per cent of the US population (2.2 million people).

> 'I have to have everything in a straight line or everything has to be in pairs. I'll put my Pepsi cans in the fridge and if there's one too many then I'll put it in another cupboard somewhere.'
>
> **David Beckham**

Obsessions are intrusive and unwanted thoughts, urges or images that cause distress or anxiety, while compulsions are behaviours that 'must' be performed to ease the obsessions, so as to reduce or temporarily ease the distress or anxiety they cause. This creates a loop that can be difficult for the sufferer to interrupt and stop.

Common compulsive behaviours are:

- **A need to check**
- **A need to clean**
- **A need to collect**
- **A need to count**
- **A need to tap or step**
- **A need for perfection**
- **A need to pull hair**
- **A need to pick skin**

Those who have never suffered or witnessed OCD may flippantly use the term as an adjective to describe someone else's or their own standards or behaviours. For example, if someone likes things to be tidy they might say, 'I am a bit OCD about that.' However, this condition is far more serious and all-consuming than this suggests, and can be extremely distressing to live with.

How We See OCD

We have helped hundreds of people who have suffered from different types of obsessive compulsive disorder. In our experience, OCD is a symptom of a life event, and the cause is a thought or belief – often from childhood or adolescence – based on protection, control, coping, superstition or fear.

Essentially, OCDs are created from a 'what if?' scenario. For example, Nik once had an OCD. His OCD was that he had to check if the garage door was closed. He would drive away and think, 'What if I haven't closed it?' This began after Nik once left the garage door open by mistake, and our cats decided to use his car as a climbing frame. The heavily scratched car caused Nik distress, and as he had forgotten to ensure the garage door was closed on that occasion, he lost confidence in himself. He started to check the door on multiple occasions, even turning around and driving back home to check it once more, despite knowing he was going to be late for a meeting.

Nik would dwell on the possible consequences of not closing the garage door, often considering 'what if?' scenarios that were far worse than the original event. These intrusive thoughts would then compel him to go and check the door, thus creating a cycle of obsessive thoughts and compulsive behaviours.

> **Someone with an obsessive fear of their house being burgled may feel they need to check all the windows and doors are locked several times before they can leave the house.**
>
> **NHS UK**

How OCDs Start

We have always been able to identify a traumatic life event –
such as a burglary, bullying, abuse, bereavement, illness or
a volatile home environment – or a small accident (like Nik's
car being scratched) as the root of obsessive compulsive
behaviours.

In essence, OCD is orientated around the feeling of having
to do something to prevent something going wrong, and
may have been created because one day something did
go wrong. If an OCD is created in adulthood, it is usually
triggered by an occasion when you were given responsibility
for something, such as house sitting, and then something
went wrong, such as a flood or small fire. In that moment
of trauma, you felt that perhaps you were to blame, or you
simply felt bad that it occurred, and so preventative rituals
such as checking were formed.

We have found, however, that most OCDs start in
childhood or adolescence, with superstitious beliefs such as,
'If I do this, I'll get good luck.' This can stem from a child's
imagination, a suggestion from a friend, or luck appearing to
be the only hope in a situation.

Often, OCDs are created when children feel helpless and
out of control. They respond by creating rituals based on
thoughts such as 'doing this will stop me being bullied' or
'doing this will stop my parents arguing'. Usually, the only
solutions their limited cognition and life experience allow for
are magic and good luck.

For some, witnessing ill health or a family death can
create the schema: 'if I don't do this, I could die' or 'if I don't
this, a loved one may die'. Similarly, after a traumatic event,
a child may fear that if they do not perform certain rituals,
something bad could happen again.

Behaviours and Solutions

A NEED TO CHECK

People who feel compelled to check may obsessively check doors, light switches, electrical appliances, taps or plugs because of intrusive thoughts or fears that by not doing so, an accident, flood, fire or burglary could occur. The need to check often arises from an accident that the sufferer does not want to be repeated, or more commonly because they have been given a responsibility and fear making a mistake. They begin to have obsessive thoughts about the worst-case scenario, because they do not trust themselves to ensure no accidents occur: therefore, we believe they are a consequence of low self-confidence.

If this is your behaviour, try to understand your schema. Complete the sentence below, then ask yourself why you originally needed to start checking. What happened? Why did you feel responsible?

Schema – if I don't check, then

....

A NEED TO CLEAN

A fear of illness, sickness or contamination can lead to excessive hand washing or cleaning of oneself and one's environment. This OCD can often be a symptom of another condition, e.g. mysophobia (a fear of germs), health anxiety (see Chapter 10) and emetophobia (see page 121).

We have noticed that many people with this behaviour witnessed a parent or loved one being very ill or passing away when they were children. This led them to question how they could prevent this happening again, or to themselves. Their childhood belief that germs caused illness or death means that now, they 'must' clean to protect themselves. This OCD can get worse when becoming a parent, due to the responsibility for keeping another person safe.

Over cleaning and over washing is detrimental to our health, as it prevents our immune system from functioning effectively. It is only when our body faces a germ that it can create the necessary antibody to protect us. This is how vaccines work. We are given a small quantity of the bacteria or virus to stimulate our immune system to produce antibodies that will destroy the intruder. Furthermore, our body already has a physical protective structure: the skin. Over washing and the use of antibacterial gels dries out the skin and causes cracks, opening up an easy entry point into our bloodstream. So, this OCD behaviour is counterproductive.

If this is your behaviour, try to understand your schema. Complete the sentence below, then ask yourself why you originally needed to protect yourself from dirt and germs. What happened? Did you learn this from someone else? If so, who was it and why did you believe them?

Schema – over cleaning protects me from

....

because ....

A NEED TO COLLECT

Hoarders persistently find it difficult to discard or part with possessions because of a perceived need to save them, or a concern that they may need the item in the future.

Some people who hoard may also be compulsive shoppers, who gain pleasure from purchasing items and feel anxious if they don't – but then they store them, often never taking them out of the shopping bag.

Another cause of hoarding can be loneliness, as collecting objects is perceived to fill a void. Taking up a new hobby and making an effort to expand your social circle could be helpful here. The need to collect can also be instilled by growing up with no or few material possessions and overcompensating in adulthood. Being given an excess of material items in childhood as a reward or instead of affection can create a schema linking objects to love or achievement.

There are conditions such as dementia and autism that can trigger hoarding too – these should be discussed with a specialist health professional.

If this is your behaviour, try to understand your schema. Complete the sentences below, then ask yourself why you originally needed to collect. What happened? What need does this object fulfil? Also consider why you fear needing something. What would happen if you didn't have it?

Schema – material items give me a feeling of

....

Schema – if I need something and don't have it, this would cause me to feel

....

A NEED TO COUNT

Counting is often done for luck, and to prevent something bad from happening.

Often certain tasks 'must' be completed a certain number of times, or 'until it feels right'.

We have come across this OCD behaviour many times, and often the cause has been a distressing event in childhood, when the sufferer felt out of control and so turned to luck as the only possible solution.

If this is your behaviour, try to understand your schema. Complete the sentences below, then ask yourself what was happening in your life that made you feel you needed to count. Why did you feel out of control? Why did you feel you needed luck, or supernatural intervention?

Schema – I need to count because

....

Schema – if I don't count, then

....

A NEED TO TAP OR STEP

Tapping things a certain number of times, or stepping between pavement cracks in a certain way, is often done for protection against bad luck, and to reduce the associated anxiety.

In our experience, this behaviour often stems from the suggestion of a childhood friend, or turbulent events such as parental divorce.

If this is your behaviour, try to understand your schema. Complete the sentence below, then ask yourself why you originally felt you needed to tap or step for luck, help or intervention. Who suggested it? Who did you copy? Why?

Schema – if I don't tap/step, then

....

A NEED FOR PERFECTION

OCD behaviour such as ensuring objects are placed symmetrically, turning tins of food in a cupboard so the labels face outward, or folding clothes in a certain way, is often carried out to negate a bad feeling.

As with tapping, stepping and counting, this can originate from a perceived need for luck stemming from a childhood trauma, or a desire for order and organisation as a consequence of a turbulent childhood. Another common reason is pressure imposed in childhood, which conditioned a need to be perfect.

If this is your behaviour, try to understand your schema. Complete the sentences below, then ask yourself what originally motivated your need for symmetry and perfection. Who pressured you to be perfect? Why do you feel you need to be perfect? Why did you originally need luck? What were you worried would happen if you did not observe these behaviours?

Schema – symmetry and order protect me from

....

Schema – symmetry and order make me feel

....

Schema – I need symmetry and order because

....

A NEED TO PULL

Trichotillomania is an impulse control disorder characterised by a compulsion to pull out one's own hair, eyebrows and or eyelashes, usually for a sense of relief or control.

People with trich experience growing tension and anxiety until they are able to satisfy the intense urge to pull out their hair. Afterwards, these feelings of anxiety are alleviated for a short period.

We have always found that trichotillomania is a symptom. The causes vary, but range from a childhood friend's suggestion to pull out an eyelash to make a wish, to frustration from bullying or low self-esteem as a result of turbulence at home.

The sensation of hair pulling can offer a short-term release or distraction from a painful situation, and therefore some associate it with switching off or relaxing. This association can lead to hair pulling becoming a coping mechanism when an unconnected future trauma or unpleasant event occurs.

If this is your behaviour, taking a proactive approach to future anxious situations is crucial. Consider practising mindfulness and yoga, talking to someone you trust, or writing down your issues so as to observe them from a third-party perspective

Hair pulling is a habit; like smoking, with effort it's something you can quit. But overcoming trichotillomania is usually a little more involved. By addressing your self-esteem issues and changing your perception of hair pulling to recognise it as a form of self-harm, you may find yourself searching for a less destructive coping behaviour.

The first step is to increase your self-esteem, by identifying who made you feel bad about yourself. This could be a school bully, sibling or family member. Questioning their motives (see page 139) is an effective way to alter your perspective. The next step is to focus on your qualities: write down a list of your positive traits and things you have achieved.

Now it's time to address the cause. What was happening in your life when the pulling began and does that still apply today? Follow this up with new coping strategies for future stressful events, including things to do with your hands when you're sitting at home relaxing – often people pull unconsciously when they have switched off.

Finally, complete the sentences below to challenge your schema, and if necessary find an alternative behaviour.

Schema – pulling makes me feel

....

I need to feel this because

....

I could

.... **instead.**

A NEED TO PICK

Skin picking, known as dermatillomania, has many similarities to trichotillomania: to overcome it, follow the steps above for trichotillomania.

Schema – picking makes me feel

....

I need to feel this because

....

I could

.... **instead.**

All OCD behaviours, no matter how exhausting to the sufferer, are originally triggered by a positive intent such as seeking luck, control or a coping mechanism, or lessening anxiety. However, by following the exercises above and the suggestions to come, you can challenge and amend the thought process that supports your OCD.

Overcoming OCD

As much as you may no longer wish to sustain your compulsive behaviours, you might see them as something that provides you with relief and control. Allowing any element of positivity about your OCD to remain can block your road to recovery, so it is paramount to change your perspective on your OCD, and counteract any positive arguments you might put forward in trying to make an unacceptable behaviour acceptable.

Recognise that the behaviour you believed gave you control in the past actually controls you today and in the future. See your OCD for what it is: an abusive partner. It holds you back, it stops you from doing things, it inhibits your freedom, and it makes your family and friends sad to see you controlled by it.

Identifying the origin of your OCD is an effective way to address your compulsions and rituals, particularly if you challenge the starting point and question whether the reason for your OCD behaviour still applies.

You may know that you no longer want the OCD behaviour, but fear letting it go.

First, ask yourself why the world is not a happier place, if superstitions are true. Lucky charms do not create world peace, and superstitions tend to lead to anything but happiness. We know that OCD causes distress and anxiety.

Next, make a pros and cons list, reviewing the evidence for your OCD. Follow the points below to help you challenge the need for your OCD behaviour.

* **Consider if you have ever met anyone who is pleased they have an OCD. If not, why not? Why is OCD behaviour not recognised as a great way to counteract bad things in the real world? Write down your answers.**

* **Search back to how your OCD behaviour started. Did it start in childhood? Was it a result of a specific event? Write down your answers in full sentences, e.g. 'Because my parents argued when I was little, I felt out of control, and pulling my hair helped me to distract myself.'**

* **Once you locate the event, ask yourself: 'What did I believe in that moment?' 'What was the perceived benefit of my OCD behaviour at that time?' 'Does it still apply?' Write down your responses in full sentences, e.g. 'I believed that by pulling my hair, my parents would stay together, but this no longer applies as they parted ways.'**

* Now ask yourself: 'Did my behaviour work?' 'Did it bring good luck?' 'Did it keep the bullies away?' 'Did it stop my parents from arguing?'

* Next, consider whether it is working today. Does it make you happy? If the answer is no, then accept that the underlying schema is not true, and that your OCD serves no purpose other than causing misery to you and others. Today you can choose to end your relationship with OCD. It's not what you thought it was.

* If the OCD was created in childhood, realise that you are now an adult taking instruction from a child. How would you feel telling friends and family that you lead your life on the basis of a child's advice?

* Finally, ask yourself if you, as an adult, would ever believe in something that you knew was completely untrue. The belief that OCD can protect you is false; choose to look at the facts to enable you to take control and have the happy life you deserve.

The notes you have made should provide you with alternative evidence as to why your rituals are futile and do not serve you. However, you may still have residual habitual thoughts and behaviours, which resurface when you are faced with certain triggers, making you consider performing the rituals again. Being aware of this possibility can prepare you to take action. Should it occur, reread your notes and remind yourself of the facts. Keep your list somewhere that is easily accessible to help prevent your negative behaviours recurring.

Since many OCD behaviours are created in childhood, sometimes you have to be reminded more than once that they are futile, with a kind and firm instruction.

When we take on OCD behaviours, we often lose the concept of normality, and no longer know what is or isn't a normal behaviour. For example, how often is it normal to wash your hands? Do not be afraid to ask a loved one for support and guidance at this time. Also bear in mind that everyone has different standards. For example, we personally like a tidy home – others may consider us to 'be OCD' as their standard of cleanliness is lower than ours. But it's only genuinely extreme behaviours that need to be addressed.

No matter how anxious your OCD makes you, know that you are not broken and you can get better. Here are some case studies that may offer you direction on how to approach your OCD, while allowing you to see that you are not alone.

CASE STUDY
Ashlea: OCD (Biting, Tapping and Smelling)

Ashlea suffered from OCD; she had to tap, smell or bite objects. She described it as 'insane'. It had started with the banister on the stairs, but now Ashlea was biting her hands, her phone, her hot straightening irons and her dog's food bowl. She knew her behaviour was disgusting and dangerous, but she couldn't stop herself. Keeping up with her daily rituals had completely taken over her life.

Her mum Diane described how Ashlea would double check things from the age of eight, making sure her clothes were always folded neatly in their drawers and everything was lined up ready for school. At eleven, Ashlea started to smell and touch things constantly. She believed that if she didn't, something bad would happen. She started biting the banister, which she tried to do at least three times whenever she walked up the stairs. Her husband Brian said that Ashlea's OCD could be embarrassing and frustrating, and described how it would take her hours to leave the house, making her late for work and social events.

We asked Ashlea when she believed this had started, and she said when anything bad happened in her family, she would blame herself. When her mum was diagnosed with cancer, she thought it was her fault for not completing her rituals correctly, and from those thoughts she picked up new rituals.

In front of Ashlea, we asked Brian whether his mum had ever had cancer, and whether he did any rituals. He answered no to both, highlighting to Ashlea that his mum was healthy without him having to perform rituals. We asked Ashlea to explain how it made sense that she had been doing rituals all her life but her mother had still got cancer. She said that she couldn't explain it.

We then learned that Ashley's mum had developed lung cancer as a result of her smoking. We asked Ashlea whether the cigarettes or Ashlea had caused the cancer. Of course, she said it was the cigarettes.

Ashlea added that sometimes she heard a voice that told her to do the rituals. We asked whose voice it was, and after some thought, she said, 'It's my mum.' We asked Ashlea if her mum would want her to do the rituals, and she said no. But even knowing that her mum would want her to stop was not enough for Ashlea; it was her fear of not doing them that was the problem.

We returned to the subject of her mother's cancer, pointing out that the doctors would have asked Ashlea to come to the hospital and conduct her rituals to make her mum better, if they worked. Then we asked how her mum had recovered, and she confirmed she had had chemotherapy. We asked if Ashlea had suggested to her mother that she could cure her with her rituals, so she shouldn't bother with chemotherapy. Ashlea said she would never have done that, and admitted she hadn't thought of it like this before.

She then revealed that she had started biting the banister as a child when her parents separated, hoping to make everything better. We told Ashlea that no child wants their parents to split up, but she was only eight and was helpless in that situation. We asked if her parents were still together: she said no. We asked if her rituals had worked: she said no.

We explained to Ashlea that the reason for her internal conflict was that she was now a twenty-five-year-old woman, following the rules and beliefs of a child who had started the rituals to keep her parents together. Yet they had split up many years ago.

At this point Ashlea admitted the whole thing made her feel silly, and she said, 'I've got what you're saying. I've let it go.'

We showed Ashlea her phone, which before she would bite continually. She picked it up and had no urge to bite it, tap it or smell it. We passed Ashlea more items that she would usually have to bite, tap or smell. She said it felt bizarre that she had ever wanted to do so, and that the urge had completely gone – it was as if it wasn't her who had done it. She accepted no ritual she could do would change anything.

It has now been four years since our therapy with Ashlea, and her life has changed significantly. Since that day, Ashlea has not had a single intrusive thought or urge to perform any ritual whatsoever.

CASE STUDY
Tash: OCD (Trichotillomania and Dermatillomania)

Tash came to see us at our clinic, and shared that she had a compulsion to pull out her hair and pick her skin.

We asked Tash when they had started, and she remembered the hair pulling starting before the skin picking, but couldn't recall what age she was.

We wanted to understand her positive intent: what about her OCD behaviour gave her a sense of satisfaction. She said she enjoyed pulling the hair out and then straightening it between her fingers. She would also pinch her skin until it bled a little, and take pleasure in picking at the scab that would form.

We asked Tash what her earliest memory of doing this was, and she remembered her history teacher telling her to stop pulling her hair out in a Year 9 class. We knew from this that she had been pulling her hair for a minimum of twelve years, as she was now twenty-five.

Tash explained that the picking and pulling were comforting, so we asked her what she needed comforting from. The only significant time she could think of was her parents splitting up when she was ten years old. We pointed out that as a little girl, of course Tash would have wanted her parents to stay together, and it was clear that she would have felt sad and helpless in that situation. Pulling her hair may have started from frustration, but became a distraction from what was happening at home, and so gave her comfort. Tash agreed.

We asked her when the pulling and picking had crossed the line from comfort to self-harm; was she eleven, twelve or thirteen? This perspective shocked Tash: she had never thought of herself as self-harming before. She had viewed it just as a habit, but knowing it was self-harm repulsed her. She said that she had more respect for herself than to harm herself.

We then told Tash to stop allowing the ten-year-old to run her life, and let the twenty-five-year-old have a voice. We asked Tash to pick her skin and pull her hair. She refused and said the urge to do so had gone. To conclude the therapy, we asked if she had any reason to pull her hair or pick her skin now. She said no, as she was in control of herself.

A few years later, Tash got in contact with us to say that she had not pulled her hair or picked her skin ever again.

CASE STUDY
Charlotte: OCD (Dermatillomania)

Charlotte was suffering from dermatillomania. She described having an obsession that made her pick anything on her skin she felt shouldn't be there. She would pick until she made small wounds all over her body, then picked open the scabs. Her partner had found her tweezers covered with blood too.

When Charlotte gave birth to her daughter, Louise, she was only sixteen and hadn't realised she was pregnant. She went to the toilet with severe stomach pains which turned out to be contractions, and delivered her daughter in the cubicle. At the beginning, Charlotte was traumatised – she didn't know anything about looking after a baby. She was diagnosed with postnatal depression at eighteen.

Louise said that her mum slept all day to make herself feel better, but it never worked. Charlotte admitted she lacked motivation and found it hard to get out of bed some days. Her partner said he felt like Charlotte's carer. Her condition was taking a toll on her relationship with her mum too. Charlotte described herself as existing rather than living.

Charlotte told us she had been picking her skin for six or seven years. When we asked what significant event had happened in her life around that time, she said Louise had just started school. She explained that she had struggled to understand who she was meant to be without having her daughter around her constantly anymore. When asked what she did for Louise, she replied that she knew she could do a lot more.

We read Charlotte a message from Louise: 'Mum, it would be nice if we could go out together and do more things. Me and Martin go on loads of dog walks but you never seem to be there. I love you lots, more than anything in the world.'

Charlotte was visibly upset and taken aback that her daughter didn't think she was there for her. We asked Charlotte if she felt her own mother had been absent; she said yes, and that even now her mum would say she was coming to visit, then change her mind at the last minute. She admitted she wanted more attention from her mum.

We suggested to Charlotte that she had been trapped in a bubble since having her daughter, and she continued to see life through the eyes of a sixteen-year-old.

We gave Charlotte a perfect peach and asked her to stick her nail into it. She revealed that she used tweezers and pliers to pick her skin too, so we gave her some pliers and asked her to stick them into the peach. We pointed out that the peach had been beautiful before but she had damaged it by picking at it. Charlotte agreed, and accepted that she was doing the same thing to herself.

When we asked whether she could pick at another person's skin or hair, she said she couldn't as she wouldn't want to hurt them. Then we asked for her view on bullies, and she revealed she was bullied a lot in school. She would join in with their laughter, because even this attention was better than none. We asked what her opinions were on mental and physical abuse. Was it right or wrong? She said that of course it was entirely wrong. Knowing that abuse of any kind is wrong, we went on to ask Charlotte why she would physically abuse herself. Charlotte looked shocked, revealing that she had never thought of it like that. She had not realised it was possible to bully yourself, but that was what she had been doing. She said that something had clicked in her head – she had known her picking was wrong, but she finally understood why.

Charlotte had wanted attention, and as a consequence allowed herself to be bullied at school. When she had her daughter, her need for attention was fulfilled. However, when Louise started school, Charlotte felt abandoned and lonely once more. She blamed herself for the lack of love and attention, and so started to self-harm.

Charlotte contacted us some months after therapy to tell us that she had not plucked or picked her skin since. She had got a new job, and had no problem getting out of bed and taking Louise to school every day.

12

Post-Traumatic Stress Disorder

I can't thank you enough for everything you have done for me. I suffered for five years from PTSD after a road traffic accident and I never honestly thought I would have my life back. I am sleeping and I'm now flourishing and doing far better than anyone expected of me. I am just so happy and everyone around me is so happy for me.

Jo

PTSD and Anxiety

Post-traumatic stress disorder is caused by a trauma. In our years of helping people overcome anxiety, we have discovered that the root cause is often some form of trauma. Here are some examples of life traumas we have come across in our clinic, and the impact they caused:

BULLYING

Bullying can lead to low self-esteem, fear of being judged, lack of confidence, eating disorders, fear of public speaking, self-harm, social anxiety, panic attacks, body dysmorphia, trichotillomania, dermatillomania, and an increased chance of entering an abusive relationship.

DEATH OF A LOVED ONE

Experiencing the death of a loved one, particularly in childhood, can lead to health anxiety, post-traumatic stress disorder, fear of death, OCD or abandonment issues.

PARENTS DIVORCING/ARGUING

Parents separating or arguing can be very confusing in childhood, and a child can feel that they are somehow to blame. Children often misinterpret a parent leaving their spouse as their parent leaving them. The child may perceive that they were not good enough or loved enough to keep their parents at home together. This can lead to anger issues, self-harm, low self-esteem, lack of confidence, controlling behaviour, obsessive compulsive disorder, eating disorders, hoarding, social anxiety, jealousy, possessiveness, depression or generalised anxiety disorder.

BROKEN HEART

A very painful break-up can lead to anxiety about starting another relationship, or meeting a new love interest. It can also lead to low self-esteem, self-harm, body dysmorphia, depression, panic attacks, social anxiety, anorexia or severe weight gain.

While you may not have PTSD, nor have been diagnosed with PTSD, we hope that this chapter will offer you possible solutions to address your anxiety-causing schemas.

Our Passion

We have worked with thousands of people to overcome PTSD from a host of traumatic situations, from terrorist attacks to armed conflict. In doing so, we have witnessed first-hand the complete devastation PTSD can cause to the sufferer, their loved ones and those around them.

When we first started to help people with PTSD, we were shocked that so many had been told by health professionals that PTSD could only be managed, and that there was no 'cure'. This grim prognosis led many patients to question the purpose of their existence. Having been sentenced to a life of suffering from the crippling symptoms of PTSD, their feelings of anxiety were undoubtedly inflated.

> *When hope is taken away from us, so is our sense of purpose.*

We were keen to help sufferers overcome their PTSD on television, and it became our personal mission to offer hope to other viewers suffering from this condition. We knew we were achieving this when we started receiving messages of thanks from viewers, who said that seeing someone cured of PTSD had given them a reason to carry on.

> *There is nothing in the world that is more gratifying than when a stranger thanks you for saving their life.*

A life saved

While attending a charity event in October 2015, we were approached by a man who asked if he could shake our hands. We were touched by his gesture, but confused when he said, 'I just wanted to say thank you for saving my life,' as neither of us recalled having met this man. He told us he was a former soldier and had suffered from combat PTSD since his tours of Iraq. He shared how he had given up after having tried all the therapy on offer and being told that PTSD could only be managed at best. With no way out of the hell of PTSD, he made the decision to unburden his partner and child, and stop his suffering by taking his own life.

As he sat writing his suicide note at the kitchen table, the television was playing in the background and the words 'combat PTSD' caught his attention. He watched as former frontline paramedic Michelle shared her story of her inability to live a normal life after returning from Afghanistan. Everything Michelle described applied to him too. Then he became captivated as Michelle related her recovery after just two therapy sessions with us. He said he wept as the weight he had been carrying on his shoulders lifted. He had not overcome his PTSD, but realised that maybe one day he could – this information alone gave him the gift of life.

This was a moment we will never forget. Meeting this man made us more determined than ever to share our therapy in a public forum, in order to raise awareness and continue to provide hope.

What is Post-Traumatic Stress Disorder?

Post-traumatic stress disorder (PTSD) is caused by a person witnessing or experiencing a frightening, traumatic or life-threatening event.

Complex post-traumatic stress disorder (CPTSD) is diagnosed when the sufferer has witnessed or experienced repeated or prolonged traumatic events, such as a soldier who has been in battle (also referred to as combat PTSD).

PTSD can also be a result of indirect exposure to trauma, such as being told about a loved one's violent death. It is incredibly common, with many suffering in silence.

Statistically, one in three people who have experienced a trauma will go on to develop PTSD, and the onset of symptoms can be delayed for months or even years.

The PTSD response is triggered when your fight-or-flight mechanism kicks in (see Chapter 2), as your brain tries to protect you from a similar traumatic event occurring again. However, the protection response becomes alerted at times when there is no danger, creating intense feelings of anxiety in normal daily life.

Anyone can suffer from PTSD, though studies suggest that women are twice as likely as men to develop the condition.

Symptoms of PTSD

If you are suffering from PTSD, you might be experiencing one of many different symptoms, including:

- **Anxiety**
- **Avoidance**
- **Depression**
- **Insomnia**
- **Anger**
- **Agitation**
- **Aggression**
- **Flashbacks**
- **Fear of certain places**

- **Fear of certain objects**
- **Disturbing thoughts and feelings**
- **Intrusive thoughts**
- **Nightmares**
- **Detachment or estrangement from other people (depersonalisation)**
- **Hypervigilance**
- **Self-destructive behaviour**
- **Mistrust**
- **Guilt**
- **Loneliness**
- **Negative thinking about oneself**
- **Negative thinking about others**
- **Hopelessness**
- **Difficulty remembering things**
- **Difficulty with relationships**
- **Feeling emotionally numb**

Symptoms of PTSD can be all-consuming. They are triggered by sounds, smells, sensations or images that are similar to what was experienced during the trauma.

PTSD is often the result of a dangerous situation in which one's life was threatened. This means that the fight-or-flight response is elevated to the highest level, and a strong negative reaction can occur to something as ordinary as a loud noise or an accidental touch.

How We See PTSD

When explaining PTSD to our clients, we use the analogy that life is like a vinyl record that's playing. If you experience a trauma however, the needle becomes stuck in the groove of that trauma, and you remain in that loop. Your life continues to play on as it should have done, however you now observe your life from the groove of the trauma that you are stuck in. This can create feelings of absence, unreality and desensitisation.

As human beings we are naturally fixers, so you replay the traumatic event over and over, looking for a solution. This creates a loop of habitual behaviour and negative emotion, which invariably causes feelings of anxiety. We refer to these as flashbacks. Although they are often unpleasant, we believe their purpose is to keep showing you what happened in order to help you find a resolution to the event, so that you can feel better about the trauma.

Feelings of guilt also frequently arise with PTSD, along the lines that you could have done something differently or shouldn't have been in that place at that time. Survivor's guilt – for the lives lost, or that you survived when others did not – is common too.

Post-traumatic stress disorder keeps you stuck in the moment of your trauma, as a victim of that event. It is only when you are able to see the event from a different perspective that you can be released, and live free from PTSD.

You Are Not Alone

Considering that around half of all people will experience a trauma in their life, it is hardly surprising that so many –

one in every three who suffer a trauma, according to The Royal College of Psychiatrists – go on to develop PTSD. This condition is especially common in certain groups of people:

- **One in five firefighters**
- **Half of female rape victims**
- **Two in three prisoners of war**[14]

Overcoming PTSD

With the right help, support and therapy, in time anyone can fully overcome PTSD. We hope that the tips at the end of this chapter will offer some guidance for you to break out of your moment of trauma and alleviate your PTSD. You may also find similarities in the following case studies to consider and apply to your own circumstances, in order to positively condition your PTSD or anxiety-causing schema.

CASE STUDY
Mo: Serial Killer Attack

In October 1980, Mo's life changed forever when she was brutally attacked by someone she believed to be the serial killer known as the 'Yorkshire Ripper'.

With her twenty-first birthday approaching, art student Mo had been out for drinks with friends, but they all left early as a curfew had been imposed in the area of Leeds where Mo was living: there was a serial killer at large. Mo took a shortcut through her university campus, which felt safe given that the murderer had targeted prostitutes.

Suddenly, a man approached her from behind. When he adjusted his pace so that he was right behind her, Mo sensed that she was in danger and started to run. The man chased her and struck her head; she crashed to the pavement and fell unconscious.

Mo's next recollection was waking up in hospital. She was so badly beaten that her own parents had walked past her bed as they hadn't recognised her.

Thankfully, the killer had been disturbed and ran away when two female students walked down the same path and screamed as they saw a hammer being taken to Mo's head.

Although Mo was lucky to survive the attack, she was left deeply traumatised by it. For years, she had only been able to sleep by self-medicating with alcohol. She often had terrifying flashbacks, she struggled with night terrors, she couldn't cope with people walking behind her, she could never return to Leeds or the hospital she had been taken to, and she had difficulty being alone in public places. While Mo physically survived the attack, psychologically she did not. Her schemas included: 'Leeds is dangerous to me', 'People behind me will attack me', 'The dark is a danger' and 'The hospital will humiliate me as the doctors think I must have been a prostitute.'

Thirty-five years later, having undergone twenty years of therapy with various therapists, Mo contacted us, desperate for our help.

When we asked at the beginning of our therapy whether she would be able to go back to the scene of the attack, she said no. When we asked if she could look at a picture of the perpetrator, Mo said that she would, but before turning the picture over she became upset and frightened. She said, 'I tried to run away that night, and I have been running ever since.'

We suggested to Mo that she was indeed a victim on the night of the attack, but now she was stuck in time, continuing to be the Yorkshire Ripper's victim. Mo agreed.

Then we challenged the schemas Mo had created, to release her and allow her to transition from victim to victor, from sufferer to survivor. We wanted Mo to see the event from a different perspective. We asked if the killer had been waiting specifically for her that night, or if he was waiting for any woman. Mo confirmed that he wanted a woman. We asked if he knew her name when he attacked her, if he had known her whereabouts and that she would be walking through the university campus at that time. Mo confirmed he had not. We also pointed out that, had he actually planned to find and kill her specifically, he would not have run away. He would have finished the job.

Mo listened, then said: 'I hadn't looked at it that way before.'

We proceeded to unpack and challenge each sub-schema she had created. Mo said she couldn't return to Leeds, but we asked, 'Wasn't Leeds a victim too at that time?' Just as the Yorkshire Ripper had chosen the women, he chose to conduct his murders in Leeds. The city hadn't chosen this; he had. Mo agreed. Mo also said she couldn't return to the hospital that had treated her. We asked whether the hospital had hurt her, or saved her life. Mo confirmed the hospital had helped her to heal. Mo had never returned to the campus, but it was thanks to being on the campus that she survived – the other students would not have been there to interrupt the killer otherwise. Mo said this was true. Finally, Mo was unable to look at a photograph of the Yorkshire Ripper, but we asked if he knew her, or even knew her name. Did he even care who she was? He was in prison for the rest of his life. However, Mo had foiled his intention to kill that night. Again, Mo said she had never looked at the attack in this way, and that she suddenly felt very strong and focused.

We wanted to help Mo make peace with Leeds, the campus and the hospital, so we took her back there. At the hospital she was calm and grateful to the staff. At the scene of the crime, she displayed no signs of anxiety and showed us around without any distress. She looked at the picture of the Yorkshire Ripper and felt defiant. He had not broken her.

Since our therapy, Mo has been able to sleep through the night without alcohol. She told us she has become a much calmer person and feels at one with herself now that her anxiety has gone. Mo, a university lecturer, now uses her art to support a charity for victims of crime.

CASE STUDY
Stephen: Car Jacking

In February 2007, Stephen went out for a drive late in the evening. Having pulled into a lay-by some four miles from home to collect his thoughts, he was subjected to an unprovoked attack. Four men who insisted they were police officers dragged Stephen out of his car and severely beat him before stealing the car.

With broken bones and a bloody face, no phone or money, Stephen dragged himself home. Despite trying to flag cars down for help, no one stopped. With every painful step, all Stephen could think about was the fact that these violent men had the keys to his home. He was terrified that they would find his house and hurt his family before he could raise the alarm.

Stephen was later told by the police that his car had been used in a robbery and was then set on fire.

This senseless attack left Stephen with crippling PTSD. As well as frequent flashbacks and anxiety, he developed a twitch, which doctors told him were non-epileptic seizures, and he was prescribed epileptic medication, which he took for seven years. The twitches ranged from small spasms to convulsions so severe that he was unable to get up from the sofa because his body was jerking so much. Stephen was eventually diagnosed with PTSD. He was told there was no cure and he would have to learn to manage the symptoms.

This dire prognosis resulted in Stephen becoming severely depressed. He would often wander off and disappear, and nobody would know where he was or what he was doing. Stephen even attempted suicide on several occasions.

In desperation, Stephen's wife Marie emailed a video to us, asking for our help. It showed Stephen lying on the sofa trying to sleep, but his entire body was in violent spasm. It was heartbreaking to see the effects of PTSD ten years after the original incident.

Stephen came to see us, supported by Marie. He described the car jacking and said that the seizures had made him housebound. He hadn't been able to work for years and he was too embarrassed to be seen in public.

He told us that he thought the jerks were a result of his body not being able to cope with the trauma he had endured, and that they were worse towards the end of the day. We said, 'So the jerking is worse at night?' Stephen confirmed this was correct. We then asked what time of day he was attacked. He replied, 'At night'.

Stephen's schema – night is a danger to me.

There was an immediate look of realisation on Stephen's face. We suggested that the jerks were worse at night because his attack happened then, and in his subconscious he expected the experience to recur.

Next we helped to condition Stephen's schema with positive counter evidence. We asked the following questions:

'Were they after you or the car?' 'If you'd walked away from your vehicle, would they have come after you or just taken your car?' 'Was the attack about you or the car?' To all three, Stephen replied: 'The car.'

We explained to Stephen that, though what he endured had been unacceptable, he was taking the attack too personally. The men were not remotely interested in Stephen; they wanted his car and he was merely an obstruction. Once they had what they wanted, they never thought of him again. We asked if Stephen feared they would come back for him; he said yes. But when we asked how many times in the last decade they had turned up at his door, he said, 'Never.'

Though Stephen was very emotional after this breakthrough, he immediately stopped shaking. A week later, Stephen told us that his shaking had completely stopped and he had started driving and socialising with friends again. A year after therapy, Stephen sent us an update to say that he was now back to his normal self. He had not experienced any more jerks and had gone back to work.

CASE STUDY
Russell: Police Officer Attack

Russell was a committed police officer who enjoyed his job. However, in 2011 he was attacked by a man resisting arrest. Russell was hit in the head and chest, and thrown to the ground in such a way that his leg was bent around a metal post. The leg was so badly broken that his doctors told him he would never be able to walk properly, or ever run again.

Russell was determined to prove the doctors wrong, and sure enough, two years later he was able to return to the police force. Russell was physically fit again, but mentally he was struggling. He didn't want to admit it to his superiors, but with his symptoms of anxiety accelerating and therapy failing to help, Russell was medically retired from the police force with PTSD aged twenty-nine.

The former officer was too scared to go out in public, couldn't face getting on public transport, and had recurrent night terrors about the attack.

Russell's schema – I am in constant danger.

He was only able to sleep for a maximum of three hours a night, with the bedroom light on. His anxiety was constant – he was on high alert, his mood was low, he would shake at loud noises, and seeing a police officer or police car would distress him greatly. Russell hit an all-time low and considered ending his life.

We met Russell in a hotel in Manchester, with his sister accompanying him for support. First we attempted to take Russell into a busy train station, but he started to panic and so we had to return to our clinic to commence therapy immediately.

Russell revealed in our session that he had been attacked on more than one occasion. He shared the stories of each incident with us. Knowing that he was now expecting every member of the public to be a threat, we began to condition his schema. We asked what he had been wearing every time he had been attacked. He confirmed that he had been wearing a police uniform. We asked how often he was now wearing a police uniform. He replied, 'Never.' We asked whether the attacks Russell had experienced were personal to him, or rather because he was on duty and wearing a police uniform. Russell confirmed that the attacks were about the uniform. We asked if Russell was the target, or a police officer. He agreed that the target was a police officer.

We pointed out to Russell that each time, he had been in pursuit of a criminal, and because he had caught them they were not attacking him; they were fighting to get away from him. He said, 'I have never looked at it that way before.'

Hearing those words, which we hear over and over in therapy, we both smiled: we knew that if Russell was seeing the events differently, he would be feeling differently too, and that his battle with PTSD was over.

Allowing for Russell to adjust to this new perspective, three days later we took him back to the train station to see if he had overcome his fear of crowded places. It was an entirely different experience. Russell was visibly relaxed and he revealed that he felt no anxiety about entering the train station whatsoever. He went on to confidently stand in the middle of the busy platform without any discomfort or support.

We have kept in touch with Russell, and he has kindly shared his amazing achievements since therapy. He has gone back to work, got married, and is now a father to the most beautiful little boy.

CASE STUDY
Mollie: Terrorist Attack

On 14 July 2016, Bastille Day, 86 people were killed and 458 injured when a terrorist drove a truck into the crowds celebrating on Nice's Promenade des Anglais. Mollie, who was on a student exchange trip, was caught up in the attack and the chaos which ensued.

Following the attack, Mollie's life fell apart. Fireworks and loud bangs would make her fall to the floor and cry uncontrollably. Anything French gave her immense anxiety, and as a result she had to change her degree course from French studies to event management.

When Mollie came to us for therapy, she related the events of the traumatic evening in Nice. Mollie had been ushered into a hotel for safety, but she said the worst part of the ordeal was being stuck hiding there, fearing that gunmen would come in. A staff member from her school was with her too, and Mollie asked her if they were going to die. The reply was: 'I just don't know.' This shook Mollie to her core. The reassurance she had hoped for was not there; she had received confirmation that she could be facing death.

Mollie's schema – France equals death.

Mollie went home the next day, but when she resumed her studies, even looking at a French book would take her straight back to the night of the attack. She told us that she could never return to France.

It was imperative that we helped Mollie to accept that her trauma was a single incident, and that she had survived. Her life had been spared, and as a young woman she should be living it and not fearful every day. After a long conversation, we finally had a breakthrough. We asked if she thought any French person wanted the attack to happen. Mollie replied, 'No.' We asked her why, then, she was blaming France, French people and the French language. Were they not targeted too? Mollie said, 'I hadn't thought of that. French people suffered and died too.'

Mollie felt angry and upset that the French police had pushed her into the hotel, and had not kept the people hiding there informed of what was going on outside, while they feared for their lives. But when we questioned Mollie about the police's intentions, and whether they had succeeded, she agreed that they had wanted her to be safe, and everyone in that hotel room survived. Mollie's perception of the hotel was that she had been trapped, and so we asked if she would have left, had that been an option. Would she have felt safer on the street? She realised that, given the choice, she would not have left until the police confirmed it was safe to do so, which was exactly what had happened.

Therefore, Mollie came to the realisation that when she was in the hotel room, nothing bad had happened to her. She was in fact being protected from the events taking place outside. Furthermore, the people guarding her and keeping her safe were French. In this moment of understanding, Mollie became visibly calmer.

After our therapy, Mollie had the opportunity to return to Nice with us. She was excited to go back, and was able to stand on the site of the terror attack. She described her change as a miracle, and her family and friends said they had got 'the old Mollie' back. The university where Mollie had been studying before the attack offered her the chance to complete an advanced French course free of charge, which she could run alongside her current studies. She gratefully accepted. Mollie has also travelled abroad numerous times since, and all symptoms of her former PTSD have gone.

CASE STUDY
Paul: First at the Scene of the 7/7 Bombings

Former transport police officer Paul's life was left in tatters after witnessing first-hand the horrors of the London bombings on 7 July 2005.

Paul was one of the first officers at the scene, at which time he believed he was attending the aftermath of a gas explosion. It was only after he entered Aldgate tube station that the message 'It's a bomb! It's a bomb!' came over his radio.

As Paul entered the station where the bomb had detonated, he witnessed scenes of chaotic terror as commuters poured out bleeding, burned and crying. Paul ran against the flow of people to help rescue the survivors still inside, having to step over the bodies of the deceased.

However, a report of a secondary device resulted in Paul being sent to the evacuated train on the adjacent platform in search of the bomb. Paul revealed just how scared he was as he walked through the train, not knowing what he was about to find. Thankfully, there was no second bomb on that train. But Paul's distress led to PTSD, which he suffered for over ten years – losing his job, his wife, and even contemplating suicide.

Paul had explored every possible avenue of help through the police force, which included CBT, EMDR and psychotherapy. His father had researched the best psychiatrist in the UK, specialising in PTSD and trauma, and took Paul to London's Harley Street for treatment. He was left crushed when the psychiatrist said, 'I am sorry, but your son is a very broken man.' Paul was told he could slowly improve and learn to manage his PTSD, but that the condition was incurable.

Before we began therapy with Paul, we took him back to Aldgate tube station to see what he felt and thought. As he approached the station, Paul became distressed. He desperately wanted to pay his respects to those he could not save, at the memorial that had been erected inside. However, he broke down and could not go in.

During therapy, Paul spoke about the 'carnage' he saw on that day. He told us that he had discussed this with therapists over and over; they all believed his PTSD was a result of seeing the dead bodies. However, we said we did not think that seeing the dead had any significant bearing on his PTSD. Our statement shocked him – he asked, 'So what do you think the cause of my PTSD is?'

For us it was very obvious. We explained that, as a police officer, Paul had seen dead bodies prior to that day, so, although terribly sad, seeing the bodies would not necessarily have been the root cause. Paul agreed. We then suggested that the one thing he did not expect to happen in his career as a police officer was to die on duty. However, while searching for the second bomb on the evacuated train, he was frightened for his life, and he had been frightened since that day. We said, 'Paul, your PTSD was created when you thought your own life was in danger. For each bag you looked inside and every seat you looked under, you were expecting to see a bomb, and you knew if a bomb were there, that could be the end of you. Although you never found anything, you have been looking for that second device ever since.'

Paul's reaction was instant. He cried, but was also beaming in relief as he stated, 'There is nothing to be frightened of anymore. There is no second device.'

After therapy, Paul returned to Aldgate station with no signs of any anxious feelings. He was able to stand on the platform where the attack took place, and described how he felt a sense of closure. We have kept in touch with Paul, and he has transformed from the man we first met. We are delighted to see him living his life, working, travelling and spending time with his son and daughter.

CASE STUDY
Victoria: Child Grooming

At the age of fifteen, Victoria was groomed by an adult who subjected her to months of psychological and physical abuse, sexual abuse and rape. Eventually, Victoria found the courage to go to the police, and the abuse stopped.

Although Victoria later married and made some happy memories over the years, she was still scarred from the trauma, and constantly felt a deep sadness and fear. Suffering with PTSD, anxiety and depression, she self-harmed and had panic attacks. She feared being alone, particularly in the shower, where she would feel very vulnerable. But the audio flashbacks she experienced were the hardest to deal with. Tired of having to cope with 'the voices' every day, taking her own life often seemed like the only option for Victoria. She attempted suicide multiple times, to the despair of her loving husband and parents.

During therapy, we suggested to Victoria that the audio flashbacks were presenting themselves in order to encourage her to find a solution to her inner turmoil. But only when she could see the events from a more positive perspective would the inner turmoil end. When we asked Victoria to think of a flashback, she became visibly upset and said she felt scared. We reassured her that she was in control of the flashbacks, and so she could do anything she wanted to lessen their impact. We asked her to alter the voice she heard to a high-pitched squeak. This made Victoria smile.

The audio flashbacks were based on her abuser's approach and his instructions to her, which suggested that Victoria thought he was still going to come and get her. We explained to Victoria that the only power her attacker held over her was the 'secret' he had made her keep: he said that if she told anyone what was happening, the abuse would get worse. Therefore, we asked Victoria to consider what the outcome had been when she had eventually told someone. She said, 'It stopped.' We pointed out to Victoria that, by going to the police, the abuse did not get worse, and in fact her abuser's power vanished. We asked her who had stopped it; she replied, 'Me.'

In this way, Victoria realised that she was the one who had solved the problem; she had already fixed it and she was in control. After therapy, Victoria revealed that she was 'miles better' and that the audio flashbacks had completely stopped.

CASE STUDY
Matt: Combat PTSD

Matt served in the military for six years, using dynamic entry into enemy-occupied buildings as part of a front line armoured infantry battalion.

After leaving the army, Matt hoped that he could return to normal life. But the traumatic events and images he faced on a daily basis had left him with complex PTSD. Matt also had several friends who lost their lives, and he felt overwhelming guilt because they had died and he hadn't. He had completely changed from the person his wife had met years before, and she wrote to us saying she was desperate to find help for her husband, because his life had spiralled into a black hole.

In our clinic, Matt revealed that every day he still felt like he was on duty. He was alert and hypervigilant, always scanning for danger and looking for exits. He had spent a significant amount of time in a tank on deployment, yet now he had become severely claustrophobic and could no longer travel. He described having a barrier around him, and pushing his family away as a result.

We attempted to peel back everything Matt had said and put it all into perspective. We addressed his survivor's guilt by asking if he would blame or be angry at his friends, if their situations were reversed and it was Matt who had died in battle. He said, 'Of course not, I would be happy they survived.'

We also talked about some of the images Matt had seen, and helped him to accept that casualties would always be expected in war. We conditioned his claustrophobia by asking whether the enclosed space in the tank had hurt him or protected him, when out in the field. Matt said that it had protected him.

Once we had systematically addressed and challenged the harrowing events Matt had experienced, and he was able to see them from a more positive perspective, he started to feel freer and lighter. Furthermore, accepting that he had always done his best as a soldier helped to lessen his feelings of guilt. When we took Matt to a tank museum, he was able to get into an army tank and sit in the confined space for some time without anxiety. Matt also flew with us from Manchester to London and was perfectly calm, even offering reassurance to a fellow passenger who was unsettled during turbulence.

A year or so after therapy, Matt's wife contacted us to say that she and Matt were celebrating their wedding anniversary in Las Vegas. By coincidence, we would be in Las Vegas at the same time, so we went to their hotel and surprised them with a bottle of champagne. It was a joy to hear Matt say that he had actually enjoyed the long-haul flight there, and that his PTSD had been cured.

> *Our past is not our future. It is a foundation on which*
> *we can stand to make ourselves taller and wiser.*

Our Conditioning Therapy

Once you have looked for similarities in the case studies above that may help you view your trauma from an alternative, more positive perspective, work through the questions below to help you deal with your trauma:

WAS IT PERSONAL TO YOU?

This is a significant element in our work when helping someone overcome PTSD, because often the feeling that a trauma was personal traps you indefinitely as a victim.

It is therefore important to look for evidence as to why it was not personal. For example, we helped Mo to realise that her attacker had been waiting for a female victim, but not specifically for her.

In a violent relationship, although the abuse may feel personal, the fact is that your partner wasn't aggressive with you specifically – they were aggressive with *a partner*. They will have been aggressive with partners before you, and will be with partners after you too, because they have aggression issues. This also applies to being bullied. Bullies are not aiming to hurt you personally, but rather to give themselves a sense of power to counteract their own feelings of inadequacy.

Accepting that your trauma was not personal to you negates the belief that you are a target, and so there is no need to be on high alert at all times.

DO YOU FEEL GUILT?

Feelings of guilt occur because you either feel responsible for a traumatic event, think that you made a bad choice, or do not understand why you survived while others did not.

Guilt is only a valid response if you directly and deliberately orchestrated a traumatic event. Knowing you did not means that you are not at fault.

Realise that, had you known in advance what was going to occur, you would never have been there, or you would have done things differently. However, you did not know, so you could not have changed the event.

DO YOU FEEL ANGER?

Feeling anger towards a perpetrator negatively affects you, not them. There is a saying that to hate someone is like you drinking poison and expecting them to die. They will not feel the repercussions of your emotions – if you have suffered, work on not allowing yourself to suffer any longer.

To do this, consider altering your emotions to pity the perpetrator. Pity the fact that anyone can be so mean, cruel, jealous or violent. To have learned this behaviour suggests that they have had a life filled with these things. Furthermore, to sustain these behaviours, they must continue to be affected by their negative emotions and their own trauma.

DO YOU HAVE FLASHBACKS?

Flashbacks will occur until you resolve the event and make peace with it. Although you will never forget a traumatic event, you can cut its negative emotional attachment by changing your perspective on it to shift your position from victim to victor. You will usually see the flashback through your own eyes. Look at the memory and imagine yourself leaving your body, so that you can view the event as a third party. Observing it as a bystander should allow you to consider an alternative perspective on what happened. You may still feel sad about the event, but you should feel less emotional about it.

DO YOU FEEL BLAME?

As we saw with Mollie, who blamed France, if you have PTSD consider what you may be blaming. What are you no longer able to do or experience as a result of your trauma? Question why that place or thing was responsible. Invariably you will find you are blaming the wrong thing, and protecting yourself from something that poses no danger to you.

We all have the ability to leave things in the past once we have accepted them. That includes old friends, former partners, careers and traumas.

13

Changing Your Anxious Thoughts

All you people who have panic attacks and anxiety like me – I went to the Speakmans' workshop and it is now at such a low level it's negligible. I learned that anxiety cannot actually hurt you; it's a thought in our heads. When you can catch it right back when it starts, tell yourself that you can stop it in its tracks and give you the control.

Barbara

In this chapter we will share our tools and exercises to reduce anxiety-causing issues such as stress and worry, helping you to attain a calmer environment and state of mind every day.

Knowing that thoughts create feelings, your thoughts can be improved by:

1   Conditioning your negative schemas.

2   Taking action to create happiness.

Lessening Feelings of Worry

Everyone worries sometimes. This is perfectly normal, and in some circumstances worrying can prompt you to take action and step out of your comfort zone. However, if you find yourself preoccupied and consumed by worry on a daily basis, it can affect your state of mind, your weight, your sleep, relationships, confidence, self-esteem, and it can really increase your anxiety.

It is important to consider the origins of your worry, and a great question to ask yourself is, 'Is it real in the world or is it just real to me?' Have you actually got lots of life challenges going on right now that the majority of people would worry about, or are you worrying about a situation that doesn't warrant being upset and anxious over?

If you are over-worrying, the question is why? Worry and anxiety are both symptoms with a learned schema behind them. What created the reference that drives your behaviour? There are a number of common origins:

* **Copying a parent. If you have a parent who is an over-worrier, the likelihood is that you will be too. Ask yourself: 'Did over-worrying enhance my parent's life?' If not, why not? When you catch yourself worrying, remind yourself: 'I am fine – this isn't my worry, it's my parent's.'**

* **Fear of criticism. For some people, worry stems from low self-esteem caused by past criticism, for example from a school bully, teacher, ex-boss or ex-partner. If this is the case, challenge your belief by asking yourself: 'Do I still want to be listening to those people?', 'What skills did they have that gave them the right to judge me in the first place?' and 'If they were kind people, they wouldn't have judged me so I shouldn't be listening to them.'**

* **A turbulent past. If there was a time in your life when a series of things went wrong, you may have created an expectation that things will go wrong in the future, causing habitual worry. Look at the evidence and note**

how many things have actually gone right, for example passing an exam, making a best friend, having a loving family, buying a home, having children, winning tickets to a concert, getting a bargain on something or going on holiday. Keep a diary and document one great thing that happened in your day before bed every night. This will start to retrain your thought patterns and create new habits. There will probably be too many things in your life that have gone right to remember, and only a handful of things that have gone wrong.

* Having too much time on our hands. Our brain likes to be occupied, and if you don't give it something constructive or positive to keep it busy, it will invariably find something negative to focus on. This can be a worry, anxiety, pain or ailment that then grows because, like a muscle that you exercise, the more you exercise negative thoughts and behaviours, the stronger they get. Avoid cultivating your worries and negativity by maintaining a positive focus.

Here are some exercises to help you overcome your worrying:

* Find the origin. When you identify what is causing your worry, you need to challenge it.

* Create a 'worry period'. Decide on a specific time slot every day that will be your chance to worry. For example, you may decide you will allocate yourself fifteen minutes starting at three o'clock. If you catch yourself worrying outside this time, don't tell yourself not to worry: what you resist persists, and it will make you think about it even more. Instead, make a note to worry about it during

your worry time. This helps to deal with a worry in the moment, and also often puts it into perspective if it doesn't warrant your time when you come to reconsider it.

* Make a list of your worries. This takes the worry out of your mind and puts it firmly on paper. It also offers you a third-party perspective by seeing it externally. Keep the list so that when you look back at it in weeks to come, you realise that a lot of the things you were worrying about never actually happened. This will give you some great positive counter evidence, which in turn will help you stop worrying in the future. Results of a study have found 85 per cent of what people worried about never happened, and for the 15 per cent that did happen, in 79 per cent of cases, people discovered they could handle the problem better than they expected.[15]

'Finish each day and be done with it. You have done what you could. Some blunders and absurdities no doubt crept in; forget them as soon as you can. Tomorrow is a new day; begin it well and serenely and with too high a spirit to be encumbered with your old nonsense.'

Ralph Waldo Emerson

* Ask yourself, 'Is this problem solvable?' If it is, decide on a strategy to solve it, and stick to that strategy.

* Consider your environment and the company you keep. The people around you can greatly affect how you feel. If you have a friend who is always anxious, they will make

your worrying worse. We would suggest avoiding that person where possible, especially while you are suffering from over-worry.

* If you would like to discuss a worry with somebody, only approach a trusted friend or family member who you know has a positive outlook on life and will give you constructive advice.

* Find a distraction or activity to fill your time positively. This could be voluntary work, a hobby you have always wanted to try, joining a local group or doing an online course – just make sure you are using your time well.

* Give yourself three to five small daily tasks that will give you a sense of achievement when you complete them. This could be something as simple as clearing out a cupboard or calling a friend you haven't spoken to in ages who always makes you feel good.

* Imagine that you have a button in the centre of your palm. Think of your main worry and press your button. As you press it, breathe in to the count of three. As you count one, visualise the colour red; as you count two, see the colour blue; and as you count three, see the colour green. Then exhale and completely let go of anything in your mind. The section of our brain that handles stress and worry has the common sense of an infant. You can't stop an infant's tantrum by applying logic; you need a distraction – similarly, this technique works incredibly well to distract you from your worry.

* Consider if what you are worrying about is a 'what if?' – if there is no solution, you will be creating fear, anger and

frustration. Pessimistic thoughts and attitudes can be challenged by directing yourself to look at a situation in a more positive and realistic way. Ask yourself, 'What is the probability that what I am worried about will really happen?' If it is low, consider what other, better outcomes there could be. Also ask, 'Is this thought helpful?' How could your worry help you, and conversely could it hurt you?

* Finally, think about what advice you would give to a friend who came to you with the same worry. Would you even see it as a problem?

Plan Your Life

In order to live a less anxious life, you need to know what you want out of it. For example, if you go grocery shopping with a list, you'll come out with exactly what you went in for. However, without a list, chances are you'll forget the main item you needed and you'll come out with a lot of things you didn't really want, which can make you feel stressed, frustrated and anxious. Life is like a supermarket of choices. Unless you sit down and plan your life, you're likely to end up laden with things you never really wanted and not getting what you really dreamed of or deserved.

The knowledge of what you want, and what is best for you, is already inside you.

The most important element of life planning is that it provides a positive distraction, and therefore lessens anxiety. Furthermore, as you start to concentrate on achieving exciting goals, the areas of your life that are causing you anxiety start to shrink as they become less prominent. The clearer you are about what you want and the more focused on it you are, the less time you have to be anxious and the more likely you are to achieve your goal. So learn to listen to yourself, no matter how much advice other people try to give you, and go with your gut instinct. Following someone else's dreams will make you feel unhappy, unfulfilled and resentful.

The reticular activating system

No matter how far-fetched a dream may seem, it's within your reach once you engage something called the reticular activating system in your unconscious mind. The RAS is like a radar for all of the things we want to achieve. It tells us when something is important to us and, sadly, we don't engage it enough in a positive way. Instead, we tend to engage it to highlight all the stuff that is going wrong in our lives.

You'll be aware of your RAS if you've ever experienced buying a new car. Think about how much time you spent trying to find one that was different and individual, and yet when you drove it away from the dealer's you started to see lots of other people driving the same car. Those people hadn't just bought the same car as you; your reticular activating system was now noticing them because they'd become important to you.

The same can work to the detriment of your mental health: if you look for anxiety-causing triggers, you will find them whether you like it or not. This is another reason why it is important to gift ourselves with positive distractions, such as positive goals.

Surprisingly, most people never consider planning their life. They get up in the morning, they go to work, they come home and they go to bed. Then they get up and do it all again the next day, without ever considering what they really want from life, or how to achieve it.

Get started today

Begin by writing your personal life plan, including everything you want to achieve. You need a clear vision of where you want to go before you can get there.

Recognise that there are no barriers – your age, anxiety, finances, education, etc., have no bearing on what is possible. Even though you may not be in a position to attain your goals and dreams right now, you may be in the future. Having a positive destination allows less time and less opportunity for anxiety to feature in your life.

You deserve to create the life you have always dreamed of. Here are some prompts to get your plan started:

* **What career or role in your current career would you like?**

* **Do you want to be self-employed, or start a new business?**

* **What hobbies would you like to pursue?**

* **What countries would you like to visit?**

* **What dreams and ambitions do you keep putting off? For example, writing a book, running a marathon, learning to drive, learning a foreign language, going back to college.**

* **What changes do you want to make in your home? For example, clearing out the garage, decorating a bedroom, tidying up the garden, building an extension, growing your own herbs.**

* **What would you like to change about yourself? For example, a new hairstyle, losing weight, toning up, increased self-esteem.**

* **What little treats would you like to give yourself? For example, a massage, dinner at a special restaurant, a makeover.**

* **What thrilling experiences would you like to try? For example, a charity parachute jump, applying for a game show, joining a drama group, learning to ice skate.**

Once you have made your list, add a realistic timescale beside each point. For example, write 'one' for things you would like to achieve within a year, 'five' for those you would like to achieve within five years, and so on for your ten, fifteen and twenty-year goals (and beyond!).

Next, choose one of your one-year goals and decide on a small step you could take to get you closer to it. For example, if you want to run a marathon, your first step could be researching how to apply. Once you take the first step, the rest will follow.

Remember to consult your full list regularly, to keep your focus on your achievements as opposed to anxiety.

Go back to your timeline

If you haven't already done so, it is vital that you complete a timeline of your life events and work to alter your perception of the negative events to help reduce your anxiety (see page 19). This is a good opportunity to reflect on your timeline, considering everything you have read in this book. Take some time now to recall and add more life events to your positive column.

Practise gratitude

A great way to increase your levels of happiness and reduce your anxiety is to practise gratitude.

When our alarm goes off, we hit the snooze button and get out of bed. We then sit and consider everything we are grateful for until the alarm goes off again, including: the fact we woke up, the fact we have a warm bed and a roof over our heads, our children, and the amazing things we have seen, been a part of and achieved.

Practising gratitude daily will help to put your anxieties and problems into perspective. If you start your day in a place of high positivity, even if things happen during your day that you cannot control and make you sad, your emotions will not drop quite as low. You can diminish the power of anxiety in your life by taking control of your thoughts through gratitude.

14

Anxiety and the Future

Thank you so much for an amazing day yesterday. I left the workshop feeling so uplifted and excited and that feeling has carried through to today – I haven't been able to stop talking about it. I feel like a weight has been lifted.

Carla-Marie

We are privileged to have worked with so many clients and cured them of their anxieties, traumas, protection attacks and PTSD. We have been practising our therapy since 1998, and since then we have seen exponential growth in the number of people seeking our help for anxiety and anxiety disorders. At the same time, mental health has become more defined and categorised, with more diagnoses and more labels being created. We are concerned that some normal anxieties are being unnecessarily medicalised, leading to a greater demand for treatment, in which medication is the most common choice on offer.

We understand, of course, that medication is a valid and necessary short-term solution to alleviating immediate feelings of excessive anxiety. However, medication will not deal with and eradicate the cause – which is why, in an ideal world, therapy or counselling should be offered too, and made available for all those who are suffering from anxiety and mental health issues.

Social Media: What Does the Future Hold?

In 2014, researchers found that people who used Facebook for twenty minutes reported lower moods than those who had browsed the internet for the same amount of time.[16] A 2017 study found that the risk of depression and anxiety among people who used seven to eleven social media platforms was three times higher than for those who used up to two.[17] A survey of 584 adult Facebook users showed that a third felt negative emotions after using the site.[18] Cyber-bullying, envy as a result of comparisons to other users' lives, developing a distorted view of others' lives, and the belief that social media is a waste of time were cited as reasons for the negative responses of participants in these studies.

According to the Anxiety and Depression Association of America (ADAA):

> **Using social media obsessively [. . .] can cause depression, attention deficit hyperactivity disorder (ADHD), impulsive disorder, problems with mental functioning, paranoia and loneliness. It is more than just the pressure of sharing things with others; it is also about how you may be comparing your life with others you see on Facebook. Many people see that someone on Facebook has a great job, excellent husband and beautiful home, and they feel happy for them. But others can feel jealous, depressed, or may even feel suicidal about their own life if it is not as 'perfect' as those they see on Facebook.[19]**

While it's clear that not enough is yet known to draw strong conclusions and there is far more research to be done, the evidence so far does point one way: social media can affect people negatively, depending on their pre-existing conditions and personality traits.

What You Can Do

It's crucial to realise that everyone posting amazing experiences and beautiful images on social media has a normal life, just like you and us. But they only put the good stuff on Facebook. Be aware that some of these posts have taken hours, even days, to put together. There's no need to feel envious, because the people in the pictures are dealing with the same daily challenges we all have – difficult bosses, arguments with their partner, angry clients, or money worries. Accept that, if your life is not as great as the ones you see on social media, it's not going to get any better by sitting there obsessing over it. You have to get out and enjoy the life that exists outside your computer – home, work, family, friends, nature, and the world around you that you can interact with as a real human being in the flesh.

Children Are Our Future

Before 2014, we rarely received emails from children asking for our help, but since then we have seen a huge increase. It makes us wonder if this is a sign of things to come. Nik wasn't aware of the word 'anxiety' until he started studying psychology; to see messages from children as young as seven who are suffering from anxiety is heartbreaking. We have also noticed a surge in grandparents contacting us about their grandchildren – as young as three – being diagnosed with anxiety.

Will we have an epidemic of anxiety in children?

Psychology Today reports that 25 per cent of thirteen- to eighteen-year-olds suffer from mild to moderate anxiety, and girls are more likely to be diagnosed than boys. The average age of onset is eleven, with anxiety cited as among the earliest of developing pathologies. Anxiety in teens and children often overlaps with depression too.[20]

'With social media, it's all about the self-image, who's "liking" them, who's watching them, who clicked on their picture,' said Dr Marco Grados, associate professor of psychiatry and clinical director of child and adolescent psychiatry at Johns Hopkins Hospital, Baltimore, in a recent *Washington Post* article. 'Everything can turn into something negative [. . .] kids are exposed to that day after day, and it's not good for them.'[21]

Philip Kendall, director of the Child and Adolescent Anxiety Disorders Clinic at Temple University, Philadelphia, agreed: 'There is definitely a rise in the identification of kids with serious anxiety [. . .] growing up in an environment of volatility, where schools have lockdowns, where there are wars across borders. We used to have high confidence in our environment – now we have an environment that anticipates catastrophe.'[22]

A 2017 briefing by the UK Children's Commissioner showed a rise of 87,000 NHS psychiatry outpatient appointments for children from the previous year, with a rise of 31 per cent among children aged nine and under.[23] These figures mirror the inquiries we receive, and demonstrate that the need for children's mental health services is growing fast.

Establishing a Healthy View of the World

Spend a few moments reflecting on your view of the world. Do you believe the world is friendly or hostile? Think about how you tend to approach new people and situations. Do you start by expecting the worst, finding it hard to trust others? Or do you enter relationships and events with a positive outlook? Do you only see the best in people? Or are you constantly looking for their faults and flaws?

If you feel that your view of the world could benefit from a change, now is the time. Perhaps you could experiment by approaching a stranger as if they were a friend, and noticing how they react to you? Or make a pledge to expect only the best from others from now on.

We have worked with thousands of people from all over the world with so many different issues, but one thing we believe is that, no matter where you are in life, no matter how badly you feel life has treated you, you can turn your circumstances around and start to get better. The key is to change your thoughts. Remember, our thoughts create our feelings, our feelings create our actions, and our actions define our lives. Therefore, if we change our thoughts we can change our world.

We very much hope that you have enjoyed reading our book, and that it has been insightful and helpful.

Wishing you health and happiness always,

Nik and Eva

References

1 Fineberg, N. et al. (2013) 'The size, burden and cost of disorders of the brain in the UK', *Journal of Psychopharmacology*, 27(9), pp.761-70

2 adaa.org/about-adaa/press-room/facts-statistics

3 nhs.uk/conditions/generalised-anxiety-disorder/

4 'Emma Stone talks "Irrational Man", the Sony Hack, and Keeping Her Personal Life Private', *Wall Street Journal Magazine* (June 2015)

5 'Ellie Goulding: I needed therapy and pills after panic attack terror', *Metro* (December 2013)

6 '"Anxiety was my prison": Jemma Kidd on how she overcame her crippling panic attacks', *Daily Mail* (January 2011)

7 https://www.ncbi.nlm.nih.gov/pmc/articles/PMC2396820/ December 2007

8 www.emetophobia.org

9 www.socialanxietyinstitute.org

10 www.yougov.co.uk

11 *Psychology Today* 19 November 2012

12 bdd.iocdf.org/professionals/prevalence/; ocdaction.org.uk/ support-info/related-disorders/body-dysmorphia/

13 Tyrer, P. et al. (2017) 'Cognitive-behaviour therapy for health anxiety in medical patients (CHAMP): a randomised controlled trial with outcomes to five years', *Health Technology Assessment*, 21(50)

14 www.rcpsych.ac.uk

15 donjosephgoewey.com/eighty-five-percent-of-worries-never-happen/

16 Sagioglou, C. and Greitemeyer, T. (2014) 'Facebook's emotional consequences: Why Facebook causes a decrease in mood and why people still use it', *Computers in Human Behavior*, 35, pp. 359–63

17 Primack, B.A. et al. (2017) 'Use of multiple social media platforms and symptoms of depression and anxiety', *Computers in Human Behavior*, 69, pp. 1–9

18 Krasnova, H. et al. (2013) 'Envy on Facebook: A Hidden Threat to Users' Life Satisfaction?', International Conference on Wirtschaftsinformatik, Leipzig, Germany

19 adaa.org/social-media-obsession

20 'The Rising Epidemic of Anxiety in Children and Teens', *Psychology Today* (January 2016)

21 'Why kids and teens may face far more anxiety these days', *Washington Post* (May 2018)

22 Ibid.

23 Children's Commissioner briefing: 'Children's Mental Healthcare in England' (October 2017)

Acknowledgements

We would like to express our thanks to all those who have supported and assisted us over the years with our mission to help people overcome their anxiety disorders. Our special thanks to all those who bravely came forward to share their journey, overcoming their debilitating conditions with our help on television or other public forums like radio, written publications or at our workshops. You have all contributed to giving others hope that they too can get better, and for many, they now have a reason not to give up.

We would like to extend our heartfelt gratitude and respect to Ad de Jongh, professor of anxiety and behaviour disorders at the University of Amsterdam. Ad identified that we had created a thoroughly successful therapy and, unlike British academics, he chose to investigate the hard factual evidence of the efficacy of our work. As a result, he embarked on scientific studies in conjunction with Suzy Matthijssen to prove the same of our Visual Schema Displacement trauma-based therapy. We are now on a journey to train psychologists in our therapy, and in so doing, help more people live a life free from the burden of trauma and anxiety.

A huge thank you to our amazing children, Olivia and Hunter, who generously allow us to spend so much time helping others, even when that impacts upon our precious family time. They are significant and integral contributors in all we do and everyone we help, through their patience and understanding of our work and our indomitable desire to help others.

You are all helping us in our quest to help others, so thank you.

About the Authors

Nik and Eva Speakman have studied and worked together since 1992, both sharing a passion to help people lead happier and less inhibited lives. Studying the work of Ivan Pavlov, John Watson, Jean Piaget and B.F. Skinner they acquired an intellectual curiosity for behaviourism and conditioning. After many breakthroughs, their studies transformed into the creation of their own behavioural change therapy known as 'Schema Conditioning'.

The Speakmans regularly appear on ITV's *This Morning* and have treated clients from all walks of life, including a number of high-profile clients. They are ambassadors and supporters of Variety, the Children's Charity and they help many people to overcome a wide range of issues through live workshops, tours, books, radio and TV.

Notes

....

....

....

....

....

....

....

....

....

....

....

....